RHYTHM

Enjoy finding your
RHYTHM

Rebecca
x

RHYTHM

Published by Rebecca Norton in the United Kingdom 2025

Paperback ISBN: 978-1-0683152-0-6
eBook ISBN: 978-1-0683152-1-3

Copyright © Rebecca Norton, 2025

Cover design and illustrations by Helen Bell Design, helenbelldesign.com

Typesetting by The Book Typesetters, thebooktypesetters.com

The moral right of Rebecca Norton to be identified as author of this work has been asserted in accordance with the Copyright, Designs and Patents Act 1988.

RHYTHM

Practical tools & ideas for finding balance, harmony and fun

Rebecca Norton

Sense of Direction

Contents

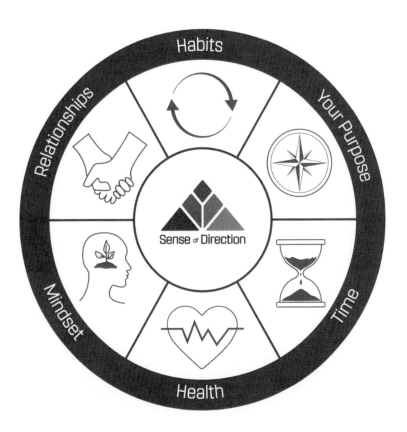

Introduction

Are you fed up of chasing your tail and feeling pulled in lots of different directions?

Are you ready to find your RHYTHM and create a life that's fulfilling, fun and flexible?

YES?! Then let's get started.

I've worked in various sectors over the years doing all sorts of jobs; mainly working part time alongside freelancing. I have many interests and I found it difficult to choose just one thing to commit to; I wanted to experience everything! This included voluntary work and enjoying my hobbies as well as spending time with family and friends. It was fine having all these interests but I always felt like I was catching up with something, or behind where I should be.

I tried different ways of managing my time and using different types of 'to do' lists. They would work for a while and occasionally I'd get the odd period when things felt balanced – like I'd finally got it. But then within a few weeks, I'd find myself being pulled in many directions. I would notice the word 'overwhelm' appearing in my nightly diary on a regular basis.

After I'd qualified as a Life Coach in 2017 and set up my business, **Sense of Direction**, I felt that I should surely know how to create the perfect work-life balance and be living my 'best life'. I felt a little embarrassed and rather like an impostor, as I kept having the same difficulties and challenges, trying to cram too much into a day or week and feeling overwhelmed.

Using my coaching skills, I started to look at what I was doing and reflect on my life. I realised I was asking myself the wrong questions and also had some underlying beliefs that were not helpful. For example, I believed there must be such a thing as the perfect work-life balance, if only I could get more organised, so I would try out different ways of creating 'to do' lists or planning my time. Looking around, I felt that other people had 'got it' and therefore I was obviously doing something wrong. I thought I needed to do everything, as soon as possible, so I could get it out of the way.

Many people talk about work-life balance as though it's the holy grail; and I can see the appeal of believing there is a perfect work-life balance. If we're constantly working long hours, or pulled to deal with one area of our lives, it can become tedious or overwhelming. We may ask ourselves, *'Is this all there is to life?'*

What I've come to recognise over the last few years

through my own experience and working with my clients, is there is **no** formula for a perfect work-life balance and it's not a 50/50 split. Sorry – it's just not that clear cut or easy!

Life is constantly shifting. We grow and develop. Our circumstances change. Our priorities are likely to differ at various stages of our lives. Balance could even change throughout the year, depending on the seasons. So it's unrealistic to expect that we can find the perfect work-life balance. I prefer the idea of creating **a life rhythm**, which allows for fluidity.

Rhythm implies changes in flow and tempo and that's more what life is like. There will be periods when we are busy and have to deal with particular situations that take up more of our attention and energy. There will also be times when things are flowing and everything feels good.

I wanted to write this book to debunk a few myths, reassure and empower you to find your own life rhythm, leading to a sense of fulfilment, in a way that works for you.

This book is for you if you are out of kilter, a busy, frustrated action-taker, fed up of feeling overwhelmed and constantly playing catch-up or swimming against the tide.

My aim is to help you gain a better understanding of what balance means to you, and how to create a life rhythm to ensure you experience life in a way that you want.

Besides information and ideas, you will find exercises, labelled **Try this**, and tips to gain insights and allow you to take steps to creating your ideal life. I will be taking you through my **RHYTHM** model, which I've developed and designed through my own personal experience and working with my clients. I believe these elements form the foundations for creating a life that is satisfying and whole.

I want this to be your 'go to' handbook for life; to come back to when your circumstances change or you are ready to move on to a different phase of growth. It's good practise to review and reflect regularly and I hope this encourages you to return to the book to acknowledge your progress and identify the areas you wish to develop.

The book is designed to be highly practical and I encourage you to underline, highlight and add notes as you go along, (providing this is your own copy of course!). You may also find it useful to buy a notebook to record your reflections and answers, so you can come back to things later and monitor your progress. I used to hate writing in books, it just somehow felt wrong. However, I came to learn that I didn't get the full benefit from the book if I didn't engage with it fully. Adding notes and underlining phrases means I can find key concepts again more easily and helps to draw my attention to important points that particularly resonate with me. By making time to do the exercises in each chapter, you will get additional benefits from the process and find it more transformative.

First, it's time to find out what RHYTHM is and how it will help to transform your life.

CHAPTER ONE

Getting into your RHYTHM

'The real voyage of discovery lies not in seeking new landscapes but in having new eyes'
– Marcel Proust, French novelist and literary critic

As I collapsed into bed, feeling exhausted yet again, I reflected on how busy I'd been that day. Yet somehow, my 'to do' list hadn't shrunk very much at all. I seemed to be working harder to stay still. Life was hard work and didn't feel fun anymore. I began to ask whether work-life balance was truly achievable; it was time to take stock.

I found myself in a position where I was frequently being pulled in many directions, wishing I had an extra hour or two in the day, or even better, an extra day in my week. There were so many things I wanted or needed to do and I still felt like I was missing out.

I was always trying to achieve a 'good' work-life balance (whatever that might be), but as soon as I thought I'd found it, it eluded me once again. That's not to say I wasn't enjoying life on the whole, but I noticed that I'd have busy periods followed by quieter times when things felt more in balance and then I'd think I had 'cracked it'.

What I began to realise was that my life had a rhythm that sped up, then slowed down or just pottered along. I started to try and appreciate the busy periods, knowing that they would be followed by more relaxed times or deliberately carving out those quieter times. I became aware that a work-life balance wasn't something static, but a rhythm that ebbed and flowed and that was perfectly normal.

I started to identify certain things that were important to me that gave me a feeling of balance or rhythm; as long as I had those in place over a period of time, I felt a sense of peace and contentment.

I love learning, whether reading a personal development book, listening to podcasts or going on courses. I noticed the same themes coming up time and again in slightly different ways and began to realise there were some essential foundational concepts that increased the likelihood of feeling good in and about life. I also noticed that it was these concepts that were missing or lacking in my clients' lives when they started working with me.

RHYTHM is the model that I have created based on my own experience and from working with clients over a number of years. It's a model from which to build solid foundations and put the basics in place. It stands for:

- **R**elationships

- **H**abits

- **Y**our Purpose (why you do things)

- **T**ime

- **H**ealth

- **M**indset

I believe these elements are key to creating a life that is full and wholesome. Once we've got the basics in place we can tweak and adjust as necessary as we grow and develop, or as our life circumstances change. See them as your navigational compass through life, helping you to set your bearings and head in the right direction.

Using the RHYTHM model, I'll help you build your own foundations that set you up for success so that you feel a sense of contentment. You will learn to identify what's really important to you and where to focus your time and attention, rather than being pulled and stretched to overwhelm. Each chapter has a core principle and will cover one element; providing practical ideas to incorporate into your own life in a way that works for you.

Let's get started

Whenever you start something new it's a good idea to reflect on where you are currently, what's your starting point. After all, a sat nav needs to know where you are as well as where you're heading, to plot a route. Reflecting on where you are now also creates a great baseline measure to monitor your progress. So to that end, the first exercise is to complete the RHYTHM wheel.

This is based on the wheel of life, which is a widely used coaching exercise. It's a simple reflection tool that gives us a general overview of our life as we see it at this moment in time. We are more than our job role or bank account; there is far more depth to our lives, and when we complete the RHYTHM wheel, it allows us to compare these different aspects. We may notice certain areas of our life are not as we'd like, whereas in other ways we are very happy. Having this knowledge can help to raise our self-awareness as well as giving us some indicators on which aspects of our life we'd like to improve.

My aim throughout this book is to help raise your self-awareness. Only when we become aware of things can we change them. This isn't necessarily easy; we not only have to become aware but also acknowledge and accept how things are so that we can start from where we are (rather than where we want to be).

> *'Awareness is the beginning of transformation'*
> – Anon

Although a simple exercise, the RHYTHM wheel is very powerful. I include a version of it in my *Starter For 10* program and it's this exercise that is usually cited as being the most impactful. Sometimes seeing your life portrayed in a visual format can be a real eye opener. Reflecting on your life in this way can be uncomfortable and upsetting, especially if you realise that you're not happy with a number of different things. However, I'd like to reassure you that it's perfectly normal to experience these feelings; to be aware of them is to be empowered – it puts you back in the driving seat. So take a deep breath and get your notebook and colouring pens out!

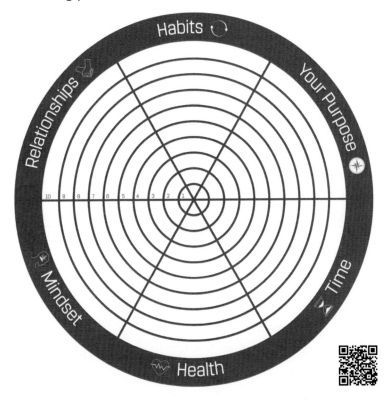

You could copy the wheel into your notebook if you prefer or download a copy from *senseofdirection.life/book-resources*. Colour in or mark out your score for each area of the wheel. There is no right or wrong, or good or bad scores with this exercise, it's simply to see where you are now. A score of 10 would indicate that you are very happy with that part of your life, while a score of 1 means that this is something that is missing or that you want to improve significantly. You don't have to show anyone else so make sure you are honest with your scoring. Once complete, take notice of the shape of your wheel – would it roll smoothly or is it flat in certain areas? This exercise can help you to focus on priorities or low scoring areas. We'll come back to the RHYTHM wheel towards the end of the book to check your progress.

Now you have a clearer picture of your current feelings towards your life, you can start to consider if there are things you would like to change. Sometimes we get used to an underlying feeling of discontent or 'making do' and forget how it feels to be our best.

As you learn more about yourself and raise your self-awareness, I encourage you to start digging a little deeper. This will help you acknowledge where you are, accept it and then decide how to change things if you wish. Sometimes 'good enough' is good enough, but at other times, you may want to aim for 'great' and set some ambitious goals.

Mirror, mirror, on the wall: reflection skills

One way of raising our awareness is through reflection, which I've mentioned a couple of times already. Reflection is a core activity in coaching which can aid our learning in many ways. It's the process of deep consideration or thought and looking at things from a different view point, which can enable us to learn from our experiences and about ourselves. It can be formal, structured and written, or it can be as informal as thinking about how you could have handled a situation in a more effective way.

This is a key skill that I will be encouraging you to practise throughout the book. To get the most from reflection, there are a few questions you can ask yourself.

⊛   What went well? What contributed to my success / accomplishment?

⊛   What didn't go so well or as I'd hoped? What factors contributed to this?

⊛   What could I do differently going forward / next time?

⊛   What have I learned from this experience?

This type of exercise encourages us to see both the positives and areas we could do with developing. We may begin to notice patterns about our behaviours and thoughts which enables us to take responsibility for our part in situations.

At the end of each chapter there is a checklist that reminds you of the key activities to try. You will get more from the book if you make the time to complete these exercises.

I encourage you to come back to this book time and again when you need a boost, to review your progress or because you've entered a different stage of your life. Are you ready? Then let's start finding your RHYTHM.

CHAPTER TWO

R for Relationships

'If I do not go within, I go without'
– Neale Donald Walsch, American author

The first letter of the model is R for relationships. It's a great place to start as it's a key element that impacts on our quality of life. Relationships can be complicated and hard work but when we get them right, they are a very rewarding and enriching experience. As human beings we are social creatures and rely on other people for all sorts of reasons.

Research has shown that connection, with ourselves and with others, is an important aspect for our well-being. Having a good network of support can help us through challenging times as well as enhance our enjoyment of life. Quality relationships are enriching and add a positive dimension to our life rhythm. Relationships can vary from deep intimate connections with a selected few, to more broad connections with a wider range of people, both of which are valuable.

Connection includes interactions with other people, as well as how we relate to ourselves. It's not only how we speak but also how we think and behave.

Relationships is a huge topic and could fill a whole book so I've narrowed it down to some key themes. This includes the relationship with our self; getting to know ourselves better, inner chatter, understanding emotions, taking responsibility and acceptance. We'll then take a look at our relationships with other people; setting boundaries, managing expectations and how to tackle challenging conversations.

Core principle: Build self-awareness, create meaningful connections and strengthen our relationships.

So let's take a moment to explore what the significance of relationships is in creating a better life rhythm. Developing a strong relationship with ourselves and our mindset helps build resilience. Resilience is a fundamental aspect to leading a life that you are happy with, where you have the energy and tools to tackle life's challenges. Mindset is the last element of RHYTHM – Relationships and Mindset form the bookends, if you will, of creating your ideal life rhythm.

Resilience is an inner strength and flexibility; our ability to bounce back after setbacks or challenges. Life is constantly changing and throws up obstacles or difficulties, but higher levels of resilience enable us to tackle these situations and experiences more easily. We each have an emotional bank account and have to make deposits as well as spending from it, otherwise we become overdrawn and that's what contributes to burnout. Having a good level of resilience helps to keep our bank account topped up. Some of the later chapters will provide suggestions for ways to do this.

Resilience and relationships influence and impact on each other. When we have good strong relationships and a network of support, our resilience level improves. If our relationships with others deteriorates, so does our level of resilience. This chapter is designed to help you consider your thoughts and behaviours towards yourself, as well as how to build stronger relationships with others.

This chapter is split into two parts: our internal relationship, i.e. the relationship with ourselves, and our external relationships with others. I'll be guiding you on how to raise your self-awareness and build a stronger relationship with yourself through looking at your beliefs, emotions as 'messengers' (i.e. what are our emotions trying to tell us – more on this later) and taking responsibility. Developing the relationship with ourselves is fundamental as it will form the basis for all our other relationships.

The latter part of this chapter will then take a look at our relationships with other people and how they impact on our well-being. I'll be encouraging you to think about the people you spend time with, boundary setting, communication skills and managing expectations.

Internal relationship – learning about ourselves

Raising our self-awareness is an essential part of learning to understand and develop the relationship with ourselves. Self-awareness is our ability to see what makes us individual; our values, passions and how we impact on others. It's also about understanding how others perceive us (which relates to the latter parts of this chapter). We have to get to know ourselves on a deep level – what do we truly enjoy in life? What are we good at? What are our areas for development? And lastly, harder to know, what are our blind spots? i.e. the things that are perhaps obvious to others but not to us. Building this knowledge base will enable us to make better decisions and improve our well-being overall.

Pause for a moment and think about what your ideal relationship would look, feel and sound like (not a romantic relationship but a close one). How would you feel around that person? How would you communicate with each other?

Now compare how your ideal relationship matches up with the relationship you have with yourself. Do you enjoy spending time with yourself? Do you talk to yourself in a positive and loving way? Can you trust and rely on yourself?

The person we have the longest relationship with, is of course, ourselves so it makes sense that it needs to be a good one! When we have a solid relationship with ourselves, it is then easier to form positive connections with other people.

Think about a time when you have presented as your best self; when you have felt positive, excited and when things have gone well, when you felt good. What were you doing? Where were you? Who were you with? What do you think made you feel good?

As I mentioned in the first chapter, we can sometimes get used to being under par or feeling mediocre and forget what we can be like when we are at our best.

Try this: Find a photo of yourself when you felt great and stick it in to your notebook or remember a time when you were at your best. Then make notes about the situation and experience. Keep the notebook close to hand to remind you of how you **can** be.

We change and grow all the time. We're not going to be the same person we were five or ten years ago, or even a year ago. Our circumstances may have changed, leading to different priorities and interests. To help us stay at our best, we need to continue learning, reflecting and being curious about ourselves.

Here are a few behaviours that help to build a strong relationship with yourself:

- Be your own cheerleader. Talk to yourself using positive and encouraging language

- Look after yourself mentally and emotionally – see emotions as 'messengers' (providing valuable information about how we experience the world and how different situations or people make us feel)

- Take responsibility for your behaviours and well-being.

- Recognise what's yours and what is not

- Learn acceptance

- Look after yourself physically

- Do things that nourish your soul

I'll be covering some of the later points further on, but let's dig a little deeper into the first couple.

Be your own cheerleader

Everyone has an inner voice chattering away on a pretty constant basis (even if you are not aware of it all the time). Start to take notice of whether it's generally a positive or negative tone of voice. Perhaps it's telling you what you can or can't do or should or shouldn't do. Maybe it's calling you names or poking fun (e.g. *Why did you say that, you idiot!?*).

If you are constantly hearing negative messages all day you can see why you might have low confidence or self-esteem. Imagine saying hurtful or negative statements to a child all the time; they aren't going to grow up feeling very confident.

This inner voice links to our underlying beliefs – beliefs about ourselves and the world around us. A belief is something that we accept as true, even **without**

evidence; or something we have faith and confidence in. Notice the part about 'without evidence'. This means our beliefs are not always logical or have a solid grounding.

Beliefs can be helpful but sometimes they can hold us back. Often they are formed to protect or support us in some way and can be helpful to get us through certain situations or experiences. However, we may have outgrown them and they are no longer serving us. Think about when you were little and believed in Father Christmas and the tooth fairy (I'm guessing you stopped believing when you reached double figures!).

We form beliefs in different ways. It could be from previous experiences, e.g. *'When I played tennis I wasn't very good so therefore I'm not going to be very good at badminton'*. Beliefs may come from the people around us such as a school teacher telling us that we would never be any good at Maths or a parent telling us we must always finish our meals and clear our plates. Beliefs are also often linked to our culture or society, e.g. women should take on the caring role in families.

The challenge is we may not even realise that our beliefs are impacting on our behaviours. If you find yourself being held back or not making the progress you would like, check and see if you can uncover any limiting beliefs. A tell-tale sign is hearing yourself saying things like:

- *People like me don't do well in business*
- *I don't have the right skills for that promotion*
- *I'm not academic enough to go to university*

- *I'm too shy to do that presentation at work*
- *I don't deserve a good partner.*

Jot down some of your beliefs in your notebook. What is driving these beliefs? Where have they come from? Are they really your beliefs or have you inherited them from someone else? Are they helpful beliefs or are you able to challenge and re-frame them?

Re-framing

Re-framing is about looking at something through a different lens or from another angle. You could try simply flipping your words around – instead of saying *'I'm not very good,'* say *'I'm great at this'*. However, the likelihood is that you won't believe this new statement so it's unlikely to have much impact. I find it much more empowering to use a bridging type of statement that includes words or phrases such as *'I'm getting better at', 'I'm learning', 'I can't do that yet.'*

To re-frame your beliefs, try and catch yourself in the act of saying negative things and swap them round. So instead of saying, *'You idiot, you can't do anything right,'* try *'I'm learning how to do xyz,'* or *'I'm making progress and getting better at...'* These are much more empowering statements that will encourage you to keep going. When you are your own cheerleader, life becomes a lot more enjoyable!

Tips for re-framing

- Practise this skill with the small things that don't go to plan. The more you practise, the easier it becomes

- Think about what you can learn from the experience to help you in future

- Ask yourself what skills or qualities the experience has helped you develop

Re-framing exercise

Here are some examples of things that might not go to plan and suggestions for how you could re-frame them.

Circumstance 1: The shop has run out of your favourite brand / usual item that goes in the recipe you're cooking at the weekend

Re-frame: This is an opportunity to try an alternative brand

You could make something different

Circumstance 2: You get stuck in traffic on the way to an appointment

Re-frame: This is an opportunity to practise mindfulness and patience.

You have time to chat with your passenger

This is a reminder to set off earlier in future, to allow extra time

Circumstance 3:   You didn't get the job you interviewed for, or onto the course you applied for

Re-frame: This makes room for a new opportunity, or a better offer

It was good practise for the next interview

Circumstance 4:   Your friend doesn't text you back and you can see they got the message. (It could be they don't want to talk to you, but equally, it could be for another reason.)

Re-frame: They are busy at the moment and will message you later

They probably forgot to reply. You could call them later.

Circumstance 5:   You are made redundant

Re-frame: This is an opportunity for reflection and consider what you really want to do

You could use this opportunity to retrain and gain new qualifications

You could use your redundancy money to set up your own business

It's a good time to find a better employer and a new job that you prefer

Now have a go yourself in your notebook...

Think of your own situations or use the following as inspiration.

- Your holiday gets cancelled

- Your car breaks down

- You miss your bus / train

- Your alarm doesn't go off and you oversleep, making you late

- You wake up in the early hours and can't get back to sleep

When we know our inner voice is fair, reasonable and encouraging, we can start to trust ourselves more. We can learn to recognise when things just don't feel right. This is when we are more able to identify different emotions and use them to help us make informed decisions.

Emotions as messengers

Beliefs can often trigger different emotions. As human beings, we get the privilege of being able to experience a wide range of emotions from rage and anger, to joy and pleasure. It's natural to experience various emotions at different points in our lives (or even in a day!). Ideally, we don't want to swing from one extreme to the other very often though, as this can be confusing and energy-sapping. There is no inherently 'bad' emotion – they all have a role to play, but it is important not to get stuck in any one particular emotion for too long.

Just because we are an adult does not mean we are all emotionally mature, and sometimes this can make our interactions challenging. Emotions can be nuanced and depending on our role models when we were growing up, we may or may not know how to express them effectively. If this is something you struggle with, it is worth getting support from a professional.

I try to think of emotions as messengers, helping us to understand our feelings and experiences. When we experience a negative emotion, it is often because it has triggered something in us or feels out of alignment with who we are. If we feel anger, it's frequently because something has touched a nerve, or something / someone has violated our values. When we experience the feeling of guilt, it is usually because we feel we could have done better. When we feel depressed, it could be because of a sense of hopelessness. Frustration or disappointment can be a sign that our expectations have not been met.

It could also be that our basic needs have not been satisfied. **HALT** is a useful, simple reminder to check if we are: Hungry, Angry, Lonely or Tired.

If the answer is yes to any of the above, then we can take action to address them first before considering other options.

Brené Brown has written a wonderful book called *Atlas of the Heart*, where she defines and explains 87 emotions and experiences. When we label emotions or experiences, especially negative ones, we are more likely to be able to process them in a productive way that can help us let go and move on. Identifying what's in or out of alignment with who we are or what doesn't sit right with us, we can make choices about how to deal with a particular situation. This doesn't mean it is easy but it gives us a better starting point.

Firstly, we need to be able to acknowledge what we are feeling rather than trying to ignore it or numb it. Suppressing our feelings long-term is not good for our overall well-being; it can lead to various physical ailments and mental anguish.

Observe the emotion in your body – how does it feel? Is it tension, is it heat? Whereabouts is it – tummy area, chest, head, shoulders? Avoid engaging with the sensation, just try to observe it without getting drawn in to it. Imagine moving the emotion through your body and out of your feet, hands or head. Using relaxation techniques and breathing exercises can help regulate emotions.

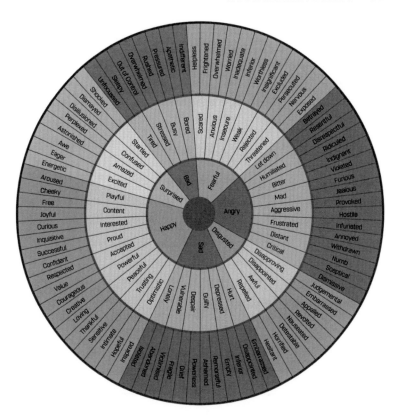

STOP is a mindfulness technique that can be helpful when dealing with a strong emotion. It creates some space to respond rather than react.

S = **Stop** Pause for a moment and notice that you are experiencing a strong emotion

T = **Take a breath** (or 2 or 3!). Allow your body to calm

O = **Observe** What is going on – how are you feeling? What is happening?

P = **Proceed** Consciously choose how you would like to proceed in a way you won't regret later

When thinking about your own emotions, what words

do you tend to use to describe them? Many people struggle to come up with words other than happy, sad or angry. Distinguishing different emotions and feelings can assist us in learning about ourselves on a deeper level and provide a way of communicating our experience. Use the Emotion Wheel on the previous page to help you identify more specific emotions.

Taking responsibility

It is important that we take responsibility for our own behaviours and feelings. Blaming other people or things for our experiences gives away our power and generally doesn't make things better. I'm not encouraging you to ignore bad behaviour in others, but I am encouraging you to think about your role in a particular situation. Do you know the following proverb?

> *'Fool me once, shame on you;*
> *fool me twice, shame on me'*

Could you have handled the situation differently? Did you choose to go along with something? Could you have addressed things sooner? The answers to these questions are not to beat yourself up with but to help you learn more about yourself and how to tackle things more effectively in future. Blaming others is often a way to unconsciously delegate our responsibility, because it means we expect others to do something about it.

This process can be emotionally uncomfortable – who wants to admit that they could have done better?

However, getting used to feeling uncomfortable is a useful skill when it comes to personal growth – in a strange way, it gets easier the more we go through it. When things get uncomfortable in this context it is usually because we are going through what I like to call, a 'growth spurt' and we've hit on something that's worth pursuing. It is much better to deal with an uncomfortable situation or experience as soon as we can. Otherwise the likelihood is that it will drag on far longer than necessary, get pushed under the surface ready to pop up again at a later date, or create an underlying uneasiness in us.

We can take ownership of our feelings by using 'I' statements. For example, instead of '*You make me upset when you show up late,*' you could switch this to '*I feel hurt when you show up late*'. Taking ownership in this way is more empowering as it puts you in control and can reduce the likelihood of the other person getting defensive as it is not so accusatory. No-one can make you feel a particular way. You could go a step further and elaborate a little more such as '*I feel hurt when you show up late because it implies I'm not important to you.*' This helps the other person understand the impact of their behaviour on you.

How we respond to an experience is often more important than the actual experience itself. There are many ways to respond. You can choose to get annoyed or upset and take it personally, which then tends to narrow your thinking and choices. You could try to cultivate a curious mindset such as '*I wonder what happened to the other person for them to do that?*' or '*I wonder how I could have handled that better?*' and see the experience from a different angle. If we can see an experience from a different viewpoint it gives us more options and tends to open up our thinking, rational minds.

Know what's yours

Most people like to feel in control of their own lives and to a certain extent we can control many things, probably more than we realise. However, we can't control other people and we shouldn't be trying to. Sometimes we want to control what others do because we feel that we know best and if they only did as we said, everything would be okay – but it doesn't work like that! We have to allow people to do things their way, even if we know it is not likely to work out; it is their lesson to learn.

Recognising what is and isn't our responsibility plays a large role in our happiness. Let go of what's **not** yours. By that I mean we have to let people take responsibility for their own actions; whether we feel they are the right actions or not. It is not up to us to control others; when we do so, we are doing them a dis-service. We take away their sense of personal responsibility, enabling them to keep doing what they are doing and we reduce their opportunity for learning. For example, someone continually getting into debt through mis-managing their money is not going to learn to manage their money better by someone else paying off their debt. Sometimes people have to learn the hard way as that is the only way they will change. I recognise that this isn't always easy, especially if it is someone near and dear to us, but we also have to be mindful of our own happiness and consider the longer term impact of the situation. This is where learning acceptance can be useful.

Acceptance

Accepting that things won't always go our way and people won't always do what we want or expect, is liberating. It may also give us the opportunity to gain new experiences or learn a different way of accomplishing something, if we are open to that – our way may not be the best or only way of doing something. Acceptance is not giving up or giving in but acknowledging a situation / emotion for what it is. We can only work from where we are, not where we would like to be. Once we accept where we are, we can choose what to do next and how to move forward. That might include reflecting how we could do things differently in the future or it could be walking away from a situation. Learning acceptance is extremely empowering because it puts us back in the driving seat of our lives.

Even if we can't control what happens to us, we can control how we respond to what happens to us. Once again, this isn't easy but it is possible with practise. Look back at the STOP exercise above to help you with this.

Once we know and treat ourselves better, we are more likely to improve our other relationships.

External relationships

To a large extent, we can choose how we think and behave ourselves but we can't control what other people think or do. However, it's worth noting that how we show up with others will impact on how others interact with us. For example, if you are behaving in a grumpy way towards someone, they may well respond in a similar way. Likewise, if we smile at someone, they are likely to return the greeting. We tend to mirror other people unless we consciously become aware of our behaviours and thoughts and choose differently.

When we start raising our self-awareness, we have a greater opportunity to choose how we respond to and interact with other people. This will help us develop better quality relationships with others that are more enriching.

When we start treating ourselves more compassionately and recognising our gifts and talents, we unconsciously demonstrate how we want to be treated by others. It is easier to set clear boundaries once we acknowledge ourselves as worthy human beings, and won't allow others to take advantage. It will become easier to decide what is and isn't acceptable to you. You'll attract the right people into your life – people who are naturally pushy or domineering won't stay around long if they can't get their own way with you.

In this section we'll look at:

- The people around you – are they drains or radiators?

- Setting boundaries
- Managing expectations
- Having challenging conversations

Drains & Radiators

Have you ever noticed how someone can alter the atmosphere of a room just by their presence?

We can crudely label people as drains or radiators. Drains are people who suck the energy out of you, leaving you feeling exhausted after spending time with them. Radiators on the other hand, are people who leave you feeling warm, positive and energised. Becoming more aware of how you feel around others can help you to make better choices and preserve your precious energy.

Thinking about who you spend most time with, would you say they are mainly drains or radiators? Have you noticed any patterns about how you feel when you have been in their company? You may unconsciously want to spend more or less time in someone's company because of how you feel around them. For example, perhaps there is a relative who you dread seeing, because you always feel grumpy after visiting them. Or maybe you have a friend who is bright and breezy and always brings a smile to your face. When we become more consciously aware of how we feel and behave, we can take action to change how we interact with others.

In your notebook, make a list of the drains and radiators

in your life; the 'drains' on one side and 'radiators' on the other side.

It can be difficult to avoid drains altogether – maybe they are members of your family or people you work with – but there are things you can do to limit or mitigate their impact.

- Limit time spent in their company

- Meet in neutral settings or do some sort of activity together, rather than just sitting and chatting

- Consciously choose to spend time in their company and do your best to enjoy it

- Schedule something uplifting for yourself afterwards

- Following your interaction with them, do some grounding activities such as a walk in nature, gardening, or taking a refreshing shower. (Grounding activities help to discharge negative energy and reconnect you with yourself.)

Our physical and mental energy is precious so it is vital that we expend it in the best way possible. Make sure you recharge your batteries on a regular basis. This is where boundaries are especially important. Boundaries ensure we remain true to ourselves and our values, keep us safe and also help other people feel safe and respected.

Boundaries

Boundaries can be physical barriers or they can be psychological – creating emotional distance or consciously not allowing yourself to get drawn into something. It may also be about what you choose to disclose or not disclose to others. Boundaries are a guide to what is and is not acceptable to you. This can help you choose who you spend your valuable time with.

Sometimes we only learn where our boundaries are when they get pushed and stretched! Boundaries will be different with different people in our lives – for example, we'll probably let certain members of our family get away with more than our work colleagues. Depending on the context, having some flexibility with your boundaries can be helpful – maybe a line in the sand rather than a stone wall – but you may choose to strengthen your structure if people start pushing too hard. It may feel challenging at first but in the long run, it will make your life easier.

> *'Boundaries; it's not about you, it's about me protecting myself'*
> – Najwa Zebian, Lebanese-Canadian activist & author

Why are boundaries important? Boundaries keep both us and those we interact with, safe. Professionals have professional boundaries that they adhere to, to ensure their clients are kept safe and to reduce the likelihood of finding themselves in a difficult situation. This might include how they behave, for example not hugging a client or adding them as a friend on social media, or how they speak to someone, such as being polite and not swearing. Professional boundaries are more formal but we each have our own boundaries, which are most likely unconscious.

Boundaries may change as you get to know someone and start to build trust. Trust is earned and created through how you conduct yourself; doing what you say you'll do, speaking to people respectfully and not breaking confidences. When you first meet a stranger it is probably not appropriate to start telling them your deepest secrets or traumas. This sort of behaviour potentially puts you in a vulnerable situation and could make the other person feel uncomfortable. However, in the right circumstances with the right people, vulnerability can help to strengthen relationships as it helps to build trust and shows a willingness to be authentic. Building quality relationships where we have trust and support is what helps to enrich our lives.

Expectations

Communication is key in relationships. Most relationship challenges are down to poor, or lack of, communication. We frequently assume that other people are on our wave length and think like we do. We can have a tendency to expect other people to be mind-readers and just 'know' what we want or need, even when we haven't made it clear or been explicit about it.

'Expectations are resentments in waiting': I heard this phrase a couple of years ago and it struck a chord. When our expectations are not met, we feel

disappointed, angry or let down. It is worth checking when communicating with other people, especially when it's something important to us, if we've been completely clear about what we expect or want. This may include time frames or who is going to do what. For example, perhaps you are planning a holiday with a friend. You both want time to relax and switch off, but you like reading books and exploring the local area, whereas your friend likes to have fun partying. Unless you discuss this beforehand, you may find yourself struggling to choose the right place to go or clashing once on holiday, making you both unhappy.

Some people find it difficult to express what they want because they fear rejection or because they don't want to come across as bossy. You can be assertive without being bossy or aggressive by using clear language and your tone of voice. Once again, use 'I' statements. Taking the holiday as an example, say *'I'd like to explore the local town and go on a day trip to see the waterfall'*. This then opens up the conversation and you can discuss what you both want to do.

However, just because you ask for what you want doesn't mean you will get it every time! Sometimes we have to accept that our needs won't be met and we may have to compromise – it's about give and take. Check to see if you are 'giving' more often, or are you the one who is 'taking' all the time? Human relationships work better when this is a fair exchange. If you are the one who is constantly 'giving', then you will become resentful, despondent or even burnt out. However, if you do all the 'taking', then the other person is likely to feel resentful, and as if they have been taken advantage of, thus making the relationship unbalanced.

It is also useful to know what others expect from you, as it helps you decide whether you can fully commit to, or fulfil their expectations. Do this by asking questions to clarify, or summarise what you think you heard them ask for. For example, 'So you're asking me to call for the shopping on the way back from work, so we can cook tea together. Have you written a list of things you would like me to get?' By summarising what you heard, it gives the other person the opportunity to clear up any misunderstanding.

I want to reiterate that clear communication is **key** to good relationships. It might feel a little strange at first, asking for what you want and summarising what you heard, but it will make your life easier in the long run. If you are not explicit about your expectations or boundaries, then you can end up having some challenging conversations.

Challenging conversations

Challenging conversations may arise from poor communication and crossed wires, or when expectations haven't been met. There may be differences of opinion and alternative viewpoints where you would like to find common ground and move forward.

The consequences of not addressing these challenges could mean they can rumble on for far longer than necessary or they are likely to resurface at some other time and ultimately, can cause rifts in relationships. This can affect levels of resilience and mental well-being.

Having a challenging conversation can provide you with an opportunity for learning and growth, which could strengthen that particular relationship, as well as others. Once the issue has been addressed, it clears the air and doesn't take up mental energy any longer.

Tips for having challenging conversations:

- If you know a conversation is likely to be challenging, you can prepare for it in advance. Give the other person time to prepare too.

- It can be helpful to set an intention for the conversation such as '*I would like us to find a solution to this issue that is mutually agreeable.*' Keep this intention in mind at all times and refer back to it if necessary.

- Ensure you choose a time and place that is appropriate if you can. A rushed conversation is not likely to be productive.

- Keep calm and notice if or when you start to experience stronger emotions. Sometimes you may need to take a time out and come back to the issue later. Use the STOP exercise from earlier on.

- Try to keep an open mind and be willing to listen **properly**. Listening to understand is different to listening to respond! When we listen to understand, we're not forming an answer in our head, we're hearing what the person is saying to get a picture of what is going on for them. It can be helpful to make an effort to see the situation from their point of view, even if we don't agree with it.

Use 'I' statements as previously suggested and avoid blaming or triggering language. Avoid saying things like *It's your fault that the house is always a mess!* Instead, you might say, '*I feel really stressed when the house is a mess. How do you think we could keep it tidier?*' You are not using blaming language and are trying to offer a collaborative solution.

Acknowledge your role in the situation.

Most people don't like conflict and don't like upsetting others, which is often why they tend to avoid having challenging conversations. However, as already alluded to, if you don't address things in a timely manner, life can get more difficult and your resilience is slowly eroded.

By implementing the suggestions and practising the skills in this chapter, there is less likelihood of having challenging conversations in the first place. When you practise regularly, these skills become a supportive habit that helps to create the life rhythm we have been talking about. So how do you create and develop habits that will lead to success? Let's find out...

─────────────── Checklist ───────────────

- ⊕ Note down what your ideal relationship would look / feel / sound like

- ⊕ Find a photo of yourself at your best and place it somewhere prominent

- ⊕ Complete the reframing exercise and practise talking to yourself in a positive manner

- ⊕ Practise the STOP exercise

- ⊕ Identify your drains and radiators and consider how to make the time you spend with them more fulfilling

- ⊕ Start using 'I' statements to express how you feel and what you would like

CHAPTER THREE

H for Habits

> *'If you always do what you've always done,*
> *you will always get what you've always got'*
> – Henry Ford, American industrialist and business
> magnate

The second element of the model is H for Habits. Cultivating positive habits is vital if we want to create a good life rhythm. They are the foundation stones of life and can either take us to success or lead to our demise.

Many people associate habits with 'bad habits' or poor behaviours but you can also develop helpful ones too. One way of defining habits is *'a pattern of behaviour regularly followed until it has become almost involuntary'*. And this is where the potential problem lies – when something becomes almost involuntary, we are not fully conscious of it and end up doing things on auto-pilot. This can be both a blessing and a curse, as we will see later in the chapter.

So, my aim is to dispel a few myths, explain why habits are useful, how to develop positive habits and how to let go of unhelpful ones.

Core principle: Create powerful habits for success and let go of unhelpful habits that hold you back

When we practise helpful behaviours on a daily basis, they become part of our lifestyle and enable us to lead the life rhythm we desire. It makes things easier for us because we don't have to think too hard, we just do them as a matter of course.

Think about learning to drive; initially it is taxing as we have to think about so many different elements and it feels like we'll never be able to master it. However, with consistent practise, we gradually begin to find the different elements of driving easier and they become second nature. It is important to note that we should practise getting into 'good' habits at this point. We need to ensure the behaviour we are practising is the behaviour we want, (no sloppiness!). I'm sure we've all heard the saying, 'practise makes perfect' but perhaps it should be *'perfect* practise makes perfect'*, otherwise we just reinforce the poor behaviour.

Some people might think routines and habits make life dull. Some can be when not approached with the right mindset, but they can also provide us with a healthy structure, leading to freedom and more enjoyment of life.

Let's take a look at some of the pros and cons of habits:

(I need to point out here that a helpful habit can still have disadvantages. Similarly, unhelpful habits can have advantages. For example, a sweet treat might give us immediate gratification to deal with a difficult situation, but too many wouldn't be good for us in the long run).

Pros / Benefits

- Make life easier, as we don't have to think too much about the regular tasks we undertake

- Filter information going into our senses, creating a sort of shortcut

- Generate a compound effect – results build up over time, creating a more powerful impact

- Reduce wasted time, thereby creating more freedom and flexibility to do other things

- Allow us to tackle big things in a smaller, more manageable way

Cons / Disadvantages

- Can get stuck in a rut or experience boredom

○   Become reluctant to change routine,
     leading to inflexibility

○   Unhelpful habits can lead to unwanted
     consequences

Helpful v Unhelpful

You may have noticed that I have referred to habits
being either 'helpful' or 'unhelpful', rather than 'good'
or 'bad', as this is a far more accurate description. In
NLP (Neuro Linguistic Programming), there is a
presupposition that *every behaviour has a positive
intention*. This doesn't mean that every behaviour leads
to a positive outcome, but the intention of every
behaviour is to gain a specific result. For example, some
people say they smoke cigarettes because it helps them
to relax. Generally, I think we all agree that smoking is
an unhealthy habit, but the smoker is doing it for a
specific outcome or positive intention – usually to feel
less stressed.

All behaviours when initially started, will have had a
reason behind them. If the outcome at the time was
favourable, then the likelihood is that the person will
continue performing those behaviours, and as we saw
above, behaviours that we practise regularly over time
become a habit. The challenge comes when those
behaviours or outcomes no longer serve us. This is
when they become unhelpful and may cause
problems.

> *'With enough practice and repetition, any behaviour, good or bad, becomes automatic over time'*
> – Darren Hardy, American author

Habits, even tiny ones, practised consistently, can lead to transformation. This is true regardless of whether they are helpful habits or behaviours that we may deem as unhelpful or unhealthy – obviously the difference is the results we get! Let's say you are feeling a bit stressed and eat one small chocolate bar worth 104 calories in the evening – it's not that bad is it? But the issue is that you feel stressed all week and so eat one of these chocolate bars every night... this seemingly innocuous act adds up to 728 calories over the week! If you do this over a period of a couple of months, you can see how it easily adds up and becomes an unhealthy habit, leading to weight gain or other health conditions. Can you think of other small habits or behaviours that can lead to unwanted consequences?

Similarly, small helpful habits practised regularly can also lead to transformative results, for example, the 'Couch to 5K' program. This is built on small regular bouts of exercise which you gradually build up over a period of 9 weeks so by the end of the program you can run for 30 minutes. What may have seemed impossible at the start becomes a reality over a period of weeks.

Try this: Take a few minutes to identify your own helpful and unhelpful habits and jot them down in your notebook. What are the payoffs from both these sets of habits?

Unfortunately, we often experience some form of instant gratification from unhelpful habits, which makes them rewarding and harder to give up, whereas the payoffs from helpful habits can take longer to experience and are therefore less rewarding initially. Later in this chapter we'll take a look at how we can overcome this issue.

Self-care or self-comfort?

As mentioned, we generally do things to make us feel good or better in some way, such as smoking to relax, eating chocolate when we feel stressed or scrolling through social media when we are bored. These sort of habits can make us feel better momentarily and perhaps give us a small boost, but in the long run, they don't improve our lives, in fact they often damage them. These behaviours are what we might call self-comfort rather than self-care. Self-care type activities might include going for a walk when we are feeling stressed, eating a nourishing meal, or listening to some uplifting music. These sort of activities can both help us feel better in the moment as well as provide more long-term benefits.

I'm not saying you shouldn't do the self-comfort type activities at all; sometimes it's fun to just chill out and enjoy some chocolate, but I encourage you to think about what you wish to gain from these activities. Self-comfort activities can become a problem if you are using them regularly as a way to deal with emotions or stressful situations. If you find yourself relying on these type of habits to feel better, then perhaps it is time to consider other options and switch your habits around.

What do you really want?

Asking yourself this question is a good starting point when you want to create new habits. By identifying the outcomes you desire, you can work backwards and come up with options to achieve them. It is important to think about what you want and *why* you want it – what will it help you achieve? What are the long term benefits or the long term goal? *Why power* is greater than *will power*, as we'll see in the next chapter.

For example, perhaps you want to lose some weight. When you dig deeper, what you truly want is to become healthier. There are a few options that could help with this: reducing your portion sizes, eating a more balanced and varied diet, exercising more or cutting down on processed sugars. All these actions are likely to lead to weight loss and becoming healthier, but rather than doing all of them at once, you are more likely to succeed if you change just one thing at a time. Making just one, or a small change feels less overwhelming and more achievable, therefore you are more likely to stick with your new plan.

By thinking of the outcome you want, you can work out the behaviours and habits you need to implement in order to get there. This is an extremely helpful tool when setting goals too. One tip is to adopt the identity of the person you want to become. So, continuing with the above theme of becoming healthy, you adopt the identity of a healthy person. When making choices about the types of food you eat or the activities you do, ask yourself, *'What would a healthy person do?'* They may go out for a walk or to the gym, instead of spending the evening in front of the TV. They may batch cook and create their own frozen meals instead of buying takeaways each weekend. Sometimes this simple mindset shift can make a huge difference to the choices we make.

> *'Habit power overcomes willpower'*
> – Jay Shetty, British author and life coach

Setting yourself up for success

Putting the right habits in place will naturally help you achieve your desired lifestyle. Hopefully, you are starting to see there are layers of habits and how these things connect. One small change can lead to other changes and the impact is magnified. That's why it is important to put the right habits in place and consider what you want from the start.

Breaking a goal down into little steps makes it more achievable and less overwhelming. If you put the right habits in place, success is far more likely to happen; the power of little consistent actions over time is quite remarkable.

When I was undertaking my coaching qualification, I had completed about two-thirds of the course and was starting to find it a little challenging to get it finished. Reminding myself why I wanted to qualify, I decided to set myself a goal for when I submitted everything for assessment. I made a list of all the different elements that I needed to do and then starting with the end date, I worked backwards. I created a chart, listing things to do each week to ensure I made that deadline. I knew that if I were to stick to that timetable, it had to be realistic and feel manageable, otherwise I'd just feel overwhelmed. Every time I completed an element I would mark it off my chart; the sense of satisfaction grew as I gradually got through it all. Having a visual reminder of my progress was helpful to keep me motivated. This way, I met all the deadlines and obtained the qualification! If I had not broken it down into smaller steps, my journey to qualifying would have taken much longer.

Another small habit I have to help with staying fit, is to get my exercise clothes out and ready the night before, so that when I get up in the morning I simply put them on and get going – I don't have to think about what I wear or motivate myself to get my kit ready. In winter, I ensure my clothes are on the radiator so when I put them on, they are lovely and warm; I then have no excuse about it being cold! The easier and more rewarding a behaviour is, the more likely we are to continue with it.

When you start a new habit it is worth reviewing how it is working out for you, and if you need to make any adjustments.

Creating better habits

Asking yourself what you want deep down, will not only help you decide what new habits you'd like to start but will also help you take a hard look at any current habits that are unhelpful that you need to stop or change. Ideally, it is best to focus on the new habits and behaviours as by doing this, the old, more unhelpful ones will tend to naturally fall away. By identifying any triggers for your unhelpful habits, you can reduce the likelihood of getting sucked into old ways. For example, if you normally grab your phone and start scrolling when you are bored in the evening, perhaps you could move your phone out of sight or turn off notifications, as this will reduce the temptation to pick it up in the first place. Or if you are wanting to eat healthily, don't buy lots of 'naughty' treats – if they are not in the house, it's not as easy to access them. Consider other snacks that you could eat instead that are healthier but still give you satisfaction. It is important to reflect on what you gain from your 'unhelpful' habit and try to preserve its good aspects, whilst omitting the negative parts. All habits meet some need, otherwise they probably wouldn't exist. If you can identify what need is being met by your habit, you may be able to substitute it with something less harmful, whilst still satisfying the need.

For example, you enjoy the crunchy sensation of a bag of crisps. Perhaps you could swap it for the healthier option of a stick of celery or a crunchy apple.

Try this: What triggers or temptations could you remove or reduce? Jot these down in your notebook.

Making new habits more fun or interesting can also be a good tip for keeping up the motivation. For example, if your goal is to be more active, perhaps you could try one of the following:

- Encourage a friend to start exercising with you. It then becomes a social occasion and it is much harder to let someone else down just because you don't feel like it. (Be mindful that you don't stop because your friend does though!)

- Play your favourite music to accompany you while you are being active

- Treat yourself to some new workout clothes so you feel good when you start

- Give yourself something specific to aim for, such as completing your local Park Run or doing a 10k race. The idea is that you build the habit of regular exercise and then will want to continue beyond the event

What would make your new habit more interesting or fun? Add your ideas to your notebook.

When we start a new habit it is like walking across an overgrown field; the first time it is hard to see a path and challenging to get through. However, the next time it is already easier to see the path as we've cleared the way a little. The more times we cross that field, the more pronounced the path becomes and the easier it is to walk over. It is the same with habits; the more times we practise them, the easier they become. If it's something specific that we are trying to learn, it's important to practise the technique correctly, otherwise we embed the wrong skill. Remember, *perfect* practise makes perfect.

Consistency is key

It is the repetitive nature that makes behaviour stick. There are various theories about how long it takes to form a habit, but my belief and experience tells me that if I practise something on a daily basis for a couple of weeks, it usually starts to become a habit. The other important factor that helps me remain consistent is to remember why I have started the new habit and the benefits I'll gain from implementing it.

Remember the triggers I mentioned above to help stop old habits? Well, triggers can also support building new habits too. Part of the problem with starting new habits is sometimes we forget to do them, so by having some sort of trigger or reminder it can aid building new behaviours. A trigger might include setting a reminder on your smart speaker, setting an alarm, putting a sticky note somewhere prominent or attaching a photo of you / your desired outcome on the fridge.

Another technique you can use is associating your new habit with an existing behaviour. For example, if your goal is to increase the amount of exercise you do, perhaps you can do 10–20 push ups every time you put the kettle on. Putting the kettle on becomes the trigger for doing your exercises. I get tight calf and ankle muscles and I was given some stretches to help with this. At first I struggled to remember to do them, but then I started using the trigger of cleaning my teeth. So every time I clean my teeth I also do my stretches. Place and time can be important factors for developing new habits, as they can help to anchor the behaviours to specific points during our day.

These things act as cues and can make implementing new habits easier. The easier things are to do, the more likely we are to stick to them and the greater the likelihood of success.

> *'We are what we repeatedly do.*
> *Excellence, therefore, is not an act, but a habit'*
> *– Aristotle, Greek philosopher*

Unfortunately, with new habits, there is often a delay in seeing the results we are looking for. So, at first, our new habit can just seem like a chore or hard work and we may start to wonder what's the point. However, under the surface, changes will be taking place and if you keep going, the results will come. For example, you start going to the gym to get fitter and tone up. You come out of the first session feeling achy or sore and your muscles are still not toned up. It's the same with the second and third visit. It's going to take several visits before you start to notice any real difference but gradually, you'll start to feel less achy and the exercises will become slightly easier to do. I think logically we all understand this delay but sometimes we get impatient. I find the gym analogy helpful to remember if I'm struggling with something new – I know the results will come if I persevere!

The key to keeping going is recognising or celebrating the little wins and milestones along the way. For example: acknowledging that you've lost 1 kg, or you've run for 10 minutes without stopping, or you can speak a whole sentence in Spanish, or you got to bed early 5 times this week.

Whatever it is you are starting to do, take notice of the progress you are making and jot this down in your notebook. How are you feeling as a result of your new habit? Have you noticed any differences in yourself or the things around you? Noticing these little improvements can increase your motivation to keep going. You may decide at the outset that you will celebrate or reward yourself when you reach certain points. However, make sure the reward is appropriate to what you are trying to achieve; such as buying yourself a new item of clothing instead of eating a takeaway to celebrate losing 5 kg!

Habits for success

Once you build that consistency, you will gradually gain momentum, and your new habits will become part of your routine where you no longer have to think about them so much. This is how you create the lifestyle you want. I also find it helpful to have strong morning and evening routines and habits. They 'book-end' your day so whatever your day looks like in the middle, you start well in the morning and end the day feeling positive.

Having a good morning routine will set you up in the right frame of mind for the day and give you something to feel positive about, right from the outset. This might include some sort of self-care activity, such as eating a nutritious breakfast, creating an intention for the day or doing some exercise. Consider how you can face challenges if you feel positive and uplifted rather than tired and grouchy.

An evening routine might include reflecting on your day, a self-care activity, some gentle stretching, reading or listening to a podcast and writing a gratitude list. Reflecting on and writing down what you are grateful for helps to focus your mind on what you have achieved or the good things in your life, regardless of how your day went. I always write down, just in bullet form, a minimum of three things that I'm grateful for or that went well. It might be as simple as being grateful that the sun shone and lifted my spirits, or having an interesting conversation with someone. I would advise trying out this simple yet powerful exercise in your notebook.

Try this: Consider what habits you could incorporate into your morning and evening routine. Write them down in your notebook.

When starting new habits, be realistic about what you can achieve and sustain. I would recommend changing / starting just one thing at a time and then adding other things in later if you wish. The idea with new helpful habits is that they need to be sustainable in the long term if you want them to become part of your lifestyle. If you decide that you are going to go to the gym five times a week, cut out processed sugar and get to bed early every night, you may find this difficult to keep up beyond a week or so and then give up, which is demoralising, if nothing else! By starting small, with only one simple change, you will see results which will help to motivate you and possibly encourage you to make the next change.

Once you have implemented your new habit or habits, you will begin to feel like you are living the life you want. So what do you really want and what's driving that?

Time to look at *Your Purpose* in life.

─────────────── Checklist ───────────────

- ⚙ Identify your own helpful and unhelpful habits when it comes to living your best life

- ⚙ Choose one or two new helpful habits that you would like to start – how can you make these sustainable?

- ⚙ What triggers can you remove to reduce your unhelpful habits?

- ⚙ Create a positive morning and evening routine so you start and end your day positively

- ⚙ List five self-care activities that you could do when you need a boost

CHAPTER FOUR

Y for Your Purpose

'Life is a journey, not a destination'
– Ralph Waldo Emerson, American essayist

The next element in RHYTHM is Y for *Your Purpose;* looking at the bigger picture of your life and what your guiding principles are. There will always be challenges and obstacles to overcome; some will be more difficult than others depending on our circumstances and stage in life. It is at these times that knowing or understanding your purpose will be particularly useful, as it can boost your motivation and determination to keep going.

Having a sense of purpose can also increase our feeling of satisfaction and enjoyment in life. It makes it easier to choose how to spend our precious time and energy as we have a deeper knowing of what's significant to us. This chapter is about *your* purpose because everyone is unique. It's not about what society thinks or your family, it's what's important to **you.**

Core principle: Identify your 'why' in life; what drives you and gives you a sense of purpose?

This topic can feel heavy at times, as knowing your purpose or your sense of 'why' in life feels like a big question. And it is to a certain extent. Some people will have a very clear sense of purpose in their lives, others may just have a vague sense of knowing and some may have no idea at all. Wherever you are is fine. I'm somewhere in the middle – I know I'm at my best and in flow when I'm empowering others to find their light-bulb moment and this plays out in different ways. Gradually the older I've got and the more things I've done, the clearer I've become about what lights me up.

I still struggle to put my purpose into one succinct sentence as my passions in life are quite broad. It's a feeling that I can't explain, especially since my sense of purpose is still evolving, but I know it includes helping others to enhance their lives.

My aim with this chapter is to guide you through the meaning of purpose and reflect on what's important to you now. This will, in turn, help you make decisions about what you do in your life and you will feel a greater sense of peace. When you know what you want it is easier to identify the things that are *not* in alignment with what's important to you, making it easier to say no to them. By the end of the chapter, you will have more clarity and a deeper understanding of what lights you up.

I've included a few different exercises that will help you think about what is important to you and what you want in life. These are an opportunity to think about the bigger picture and be creative; they can be fun and empowering. Take your time to do them and come back to them or add to them as and when you are ready.

Try this: *The Rocking Chair Test.* This is a simple visualisation exercise that encourages you to imagine yourself in old age reminiscing about your life.

Find a comfy spot and close your eyes. Now go forward in time to when you are 80 or 90 years old and imagine yourself telling someone about your life adventures and experiences. What stands out to you? What have you accomplished? What did you get up to and who did you spend time with? You can go into as much detail as you wish with this exercise. Once you've spent time visualising and imagining, open your eyes and make a note of all the key points that came up for you. How similar or different are those circumstances to what you are currently doing? What could you start doing now to make these things a reality?

Sometimes, doing simple exercises like this can give us the push we need to start taking action, or other times, things might happen to us that cause us to reflect and take stock. These can be described as 'push' and 'pull' factors. Let me explain what these are.

Push / Pull

There are certain experiences that can help to trigger a desire to change our habits. It might be a particular situation that gives us a wake-up call, or it might be that we get so fed up with our current circumstances that we consciously choose to embark on a journey to improve things.

A *push* factor is something that makes us want to *move away* from a particular experience. For example, being made redundant might be the catalyst to decide to change career, or you have a health scare and are strongly encouraged by medical professionals to change your lifestyle. These types of situations can be a good way of getting started on making changes, as there are likely to be unpleasant consequences if we don't.

However, they may not always be strong enough to keep us going longer term. For example, perhaps you've been warned that you are pre-diabetic and should change your diet. You make some changes and work hard to reduce your risk, but once you're at that point, you start to relax again and things gradually begin to slip back to how they were. This is where pull factors can be more powerful and keep you going longer term.

A *pull* factor is something that we want to *move towards*. This might include wanting to train for a marathon which is raising funds for a particular cause that is close to your heart, losing weight and toning up so you can fit comfortably into your wedding dress or suit, or getting fitter so you can keep up with your young children or grandchildren.

We can see the big rewards when we are moving towards our goal. There is often a stronger or deeper reason behind wanting to change when we have a pull factor. Having a strong 'why' or reason for doing something is more likely to help keep us going when things get tough, which they usually do at some point. You can see the bigger picture and have a strong determination to continue, despite any hardships.

Sometimes, a push factor can be a great kick-start to get us to change direction; the trick is then to find a pull factor to work towards to ensure longer term success. This can be easier once you start to see the benefits of making those initial changes, as it helps to build motivation and momentum.

These push and pull factors can hold more weight for us depending on our priorities, which are likely to change depending on what stage in life we are. What drives you to get out of bed in your twenties is likely to be quite different to what you feel excited about in your thirties or forties. There may be a similar theme but it could show up differently and this is worth remembering, especially if you are starting to feel lacklustre about life and wondering is this all there is? Checking in with yourself periodically to reflect on what you are doing and why, can be helpful to ensure you stay on track with what you want in life, particularly if your circumstances change. As mentioned above, when you know what your priorities are, it's easier to make decisions about where to invest your time and energy (we'll discuss this further in the next chapter on Time).

It's also worth recognising that what drives you to get out of bed in a morning might be different to what lights you up and makes you sparkle or excited about life. You might get up to go to work to earn money to pay the bills, but your job is not something you feel particularly passionate about. You would probably find it easier to get out of bed to go and do something that makes your heart sing. I tend to differentiate these things as 'little why's' and 'big why's'.

> *'Without a clear destination in view, the*
> *challenges on the journey seem pointless'*
> – Michael Hyatt, American author

Little Why and Big Why

A little 'why' is the reason behind doing the smaller, everyday tasks such as wanting to eat healthily because your health is important to you. Another little 'why' might be sitting down to study each week because you want to pass your qualification. Sometimes the little 'why's help us to achieve short term goals. Look back at the last chapter about habits. When we start a new habit, identifying the why behind it can be a powerful aid to keeping going with it. Why power is stronger than willpower!

There are often many things that we'd like to do or change, but it's unlikely that we'll do them or stick to them if we don't have a strong reason to do so. I have wanted to learn to play the ukulele for a long time, so during lockdown I decided to get myself one. I was trying to teach myself by watching videos and reading instructions; it was incredibly challenging as I don't have any musical background and had never done anything like it before. I practised for a while but didn't keep it up because the motivation just wasn't there. I had to accept that it's not the right time for me, as I had too many other things that rank higher on my priority list – and that's okay. We'll delve a little deeper into this in the next chapter about time.

The other thing you may come to realise when considering why you are doing something, is that it is someone else's 'why' rather than your own! Perhaps you've taken something on board because you feel you *should* rather than because you *want* to; this can be a nudge to review whether you want to continue or whether it is something you can drop.

A big 'why' is the deeper reason behind our actions and the way we live our life. Perhaps we go into a particular profession because we want to make a difference. Or we spend our time fundraising for a specific cause because we've been affected by an experience and we want to do our part. A big 'why' can be our guiding compass in life that steers us in the right direction. It is more about our longer term vision for life. A big 'why' helps us to consider how we want to live our life, what we want to accomplish and what legacy we want to leave behind. Again, this might seem like a deep question that you don't really know the answer to or have never considered before.

It can feel a little scary to address some of these questions but I encourage you to give them some thought as it can help with life choices.

Try this: Following on from the *Rocking Chair Test* earlier which is about *your* experience of life, here are two exercises that are more about the impact you and your life has on others and the world around you; *Celebration of Life* and *Life Mission Statement.*

Celebration of Life: Think of this as your eulogy or, for those of you who remember, your own *This is Your Life* red book. This is a celebration of your life and all the experiences you've had, read out by a good friend. How do you want to be remembered by the people around you? What legacy do you want to leave? What will have been your accomplishments? What stands out?

You might start by just jotting down your initial thoughts and then pondering over the questions for a few days. Addressing these questions gives you the opportunity to consider deeply what's important to you and how you want to live your life. It can be an extremely powerful exercise – either a good wake-up call if change is needed, or a reassuring confirmation that you are living as you wish. Remember – it is **never too late** to start making changes if you are unhappy.

Life Mission Statement: This exercise is similar to the one above but might feel slightly less emotional as you are setting an intention for how you want your life to look going forward, rather than looking back over your life. Think of you and your life as an organisation or business and consider what your overarching purpose is; define your goals and values.

For example, perhaps your mission is to live in a way that limits the impact on the environment. Your goals might be to recycle, reuse and reduce consumption as much as possible. Your values might include responsibility, resourcefulness and contribution. This mission statement could influence how you travel, your shopping habits and the type of activities you engage in.

Both of the above exercises are an extremely helpful way to identify your key values in life.

Values

A value is something that you deem important, perhaps linked to the principles and standards that guide you. They are usually just one word, such as integrity or freedom. Normally we have some key values that are important to us; these could be linked to our culture, upbringing or experiences. We might not be fully conscious of our values but we are likely to feel discomfort or stress if they are being compromised or not being met. This could be because we've gone off track or the people around us do not have the same values as us.

What is tricky is that you and I may list the same word / value as being important but they could mean different things to each of us. For example, we may both list freedom as one of our key values. Freedom to me is about having the flexibility to work in my own way and do the things I want; whereas for you that could be about financial freedom and having the money to provide for your family without worrying. When I'm working with individual clients, we spend a good deal of time identifying and defining what their values are as this influences the choices they make and how to move forward.

By being very clear about what a value means to us, we can pursue the right things; the things that lead to us feeling happier and content. For example, when you are applying to work for a company or organisation, there are a number of factors to consider besides whether you have the appropriate skills and experience. This could include:

⊕   Your 'little why' – perhaps you want to save money to buy your own house and the job pays well

⊕   Your 'big why' – it is an industry that you are particularly interested in, where you feel you could make a difference

⊕   The company values – are they in alignment with your own values? Do you like how they operate their business?

If you are clear about these things before starting the job, you are more likely to feel satisfied with your decision. On the contrary, you might not like the way an organisation operates and feel that you could offer a better service. So instead, you try and find a different organisation that's more in alignment with your values, or even decide to set up your own business.

Sometimes when things don't feel right, it could be that your values are being compromised or are in conflict. Perhaps you have strong values around family and money. You want to spend good quality time with your family and provide for them, but you find yourself having to work long hours to make a decent living so you don't see your family as much as you would like. When you start to unpick these things it allows you to come up with alternatives and find solutions. Options could include finding work that pays more, swapping to a job that is nearer home so you spend less time commuting, setting up your own business to allow greater flexibility and perhaps involves your family, or reassessing your budget so you don't need to earn as much money and can work less hours.

Try this: Take a look at the list of values on pages 76–77 and highlight the ones that are important to you. Aim for a maximum of ten and note these down in your notebook. Take a look at the ones you have selected and narrow that list down to between three and five values that are the most important ones to you. Now have a go at describing what these values mean to you.

Once you have an idea of your key values and what they mean to you, it is easier to start to become more aware of your choices and actions. As well as jotting them down in your notebook, write them on a sticky note and place them somewhere prominent, as a helpful reminder.

You could also incorporate them into a vision board, which is another useful activity for helping you express your desires in life. Creating a vision board can be great fun and you can involve other key people if it feels appropriate, such as your partner or children. Get a large piece of card then cover it with clippings, pictures, photos, tickets – anything that reminds you about what you want in life or what's important to you. Place the board somewhere prominent so you'll see a visual prompt on a daily basis.

The idea behind the exercises in this chapter is to help you become more consciously aware of how you would ideally like to live your life. Not everything you do has to have a purpose or be meaningful. Maybe you don't particularly enjoy your job or find it fulfilling but on the other hand, it meets your current needs and you get a sense of meaning from the activities you do outside of work. These sorts of exercises enable you to check how near or far off you are to living your ideal life; sometimes we get pulled off course by other factors without realising.

Now might be a good time to go back and look at your RHYTHM wheel in your notes from Chapter One. How satisfied are you with each element on the wheel? We have one shot at this life! It is not a dress rehearsal, so don't hold yourself back!

If you continue living your life the way you are now, will you be happy in 12 months? How about in three years, five years or longer? Do you feel like you are heading in the direction that you are content with? If you are, that's brilliant; keep doing what you're doing. If you are not, now is the time to start making some adjustments. I don't want you to feel deflated if things are not as you would like – sometimes when we hold up the mirror we don't like what we see looking back at us. The whole point of doing these exercises is to give you an opportunity to change things that aren't working or that you don't like.

We have to be honest with ourselves about where we are, acknowledge the situation and accept it before we can start working towards what we truly want. A sat nav needs to know where it is starting from to plan the route. This might be quite uncomfortable and bring up lots of conflicting emotions; not many people like to admit that they are struggling or are unhappy in their life. However, it is worth working through this to help you to lead the life you want, otherwise you may end up regretting your choices, or even worse, become resentful of the people around you. Rather than trying to change everything at once or making big drastic decisions, it can be easier to start with one or two small steps – take a look back to the habits chapter.

Sometimes when we start making changes it is not only us who notice the difference; our friends and family might start to see a difference in us too. This can go either way. The people closest to us can be very supportive and encouraging and enjoy seeing us flourish. Or, they may feel slightly threatened by the 'new' you and feel like they are being pushed out. Not everyone likes changing the status quo. Consider how you can bring them along on your new adventure or be prepared to have some open discussions with them about where you want to go in life.

Remember, I said that awareness is the beginning of transformation: hopefully now you are a little more aware, you can start making small changes to the way you do things and how you spend your time.

─────────────── Checklist ───────────────

⊚ Have a go at the *Rocking Chair Test*

⊚ Take some time to ponder on and create
   your *Celebration of Life* and your *Life Mission
   Statement*

⊚ Complete the *Values* exercise

⊚ Have fun creating a vision board

⊚ Check back to your RHYTHM wheel notes –
   would you alter any of your scores now?

Values List (Your Purpose)

vitality

choice

family

acceptance

abundance

challenge   compassion

intuition

passion

fairness

courage   power   determination

well-being

openness

kindness

connection

resourcefulness

reliability

excellence

uniqueness   health

learning

inner strength

humility

faith

truth

recognition

achievement

integrity   love

contribution

responsibility

self-belief   humour

innovation   respect

forgiveness

friendship

fame

community

empathy   trust

freedom

success

resilience

serenity   adventure

spirituality

wisdom

cooperation

stability

joy

caring

growth

honesty

companionship

creativity

wealth

comfort

personal development

balance

independence

nurturing

loyalty

decisiveness   control

commitment

ambition

appreciation

competitiveness

tolerance

hardworking

variety

dependability

belonging

helpfulness

patience

equality

excitement

capability

purpose

confidence

dignity

calmness

understanding

inner peace

positivity

structure

knowledge

intelligence

tradition

harmony

contentment

pleasure

simplicity

authenticity

professionalism

security

CHAPTER FIVE

T for Time

'The best way to predict the future is to create it'
Abraham Lincoln,16th US President

Time is a human construct that helps to create order and structure in our lives. Time can give us a sense of freedom, or if we are time poor, it becomes a barrier to doing the things we want. We each get the same 24 hours (or 86,400 seconds!) in a day; it's how we use them that makes the difference.

There are numerous time-management tools and skills but if you haven't first identified the right activities on which to spend your time, no amount of management will give you what you are looking for. In one of my workshops, *'How to Make Time for Everything'*, we dig a little deeper into what 'everything' means to an individual. When you get the foundations in place (i.e. identifying the right activities), then it becomes easier to find or create the time needed.

Time is our most precious asset; once it's gone we can't get it back, which is why it is more valuable than money. If we lose money, we can generate more, whereas we can't generate more time!

Core principle: Investing your time wisely leads to a fulfilling life

In this chapter you'll start to see how all the elements of RHYTHM weave together. I will include a couple of tools that I find helpful for managing time but first there are a few other aspects that we need to consider. When we are thinking about how we spend time, we need to be looking at daily habits and routines as well as long-term planning. If we are intentional about the former, then the latter becomes easier.

Where does time go?

Before we start trying to use our time more effectively, it can be useful to work out what we currently do with our time.

Have you ever felt like time speeds up or slows down? When we do something we love and are enjoying ourselves, it can feel like an hour has passed in the blink of an eye. On the other hand, if you are doing something you find boring or dislike, the time often drags. I did a short stint as an exam invigilator and I'd look at the clock in dismay as only 5 minutes had passed when it felt like 35! However, when I'm delivering coaching walks or workshops, I'm sometimes taken by surprise when I realise I only have 10 minutes left at the end of the session as a couple of hours have flown by.

Time can be deceptive – what we think will take only 10 minutes can take much longer and vice versa. It can be an extremely helpful exercise to track the time taken for the activities that you do on a regular basis, so you can more accurately schedule time to complete it.

Try this: Create a time log in your notebook for at least one day, preferably three if you can stick with it, and ideally include one work or regular day and one day off / weekend. From the moment you wake up, record every single activity you do, and how long it takes you. Use the template opposite as a guide or download a copy from *senseofdirection.life/book-resources*.

I know this exercise may seem a little tedious but it is very insightful. You may notice activities that are taking up large amounts of your time (possibly more than you thought!), maybe some activities aren't taking as long as you thought and perhaps there are some points in your day where you could be using your time differently. It is a good way to spot patterns and take notice of the type of activities you are doing. Avoid just writing 'work' – be as specific as you can, e.g. checking emails, making phone calls, travelling, in meetings and so on. Again, this will help identify where you can be more efficient with your time.

The other element to consider from your time log, is to look at how much time you spend on the priorities you identified in the previous chapter. If you identified being active and healthy as being important to you, how much time and what sort of activities are you doing that are active or healthy? Likewise, if you feel that family is one of your key values, how much time are you spending with your family?

 Time Log: Fill in with as much detail as possible. Preferably 1 work/regular day and 1 day off/weekend

Time	Day 1 Activity	Day 2 Activity	Day 3 Activity
06:00			
07:00			
08:00			
09:00			
10:00			
11:00			
12:00			
13:00			
14:00			
15:00			
16:00			
17:00			
18:00			
19:00			
20:00			
21:00			
22:00			
23:00			

By becoming more aware of how you currently spend your time, you can begin to change your behaviours and make different choices. You may start to realise or notice that it's not necessarily a lack of time that's stopping you from doing certain things, but something else.

What's really stopping you?

Have you ever had things on your 'to do' list that just keep getting pushed down the list and never seem to get ticked off? Although it is convenient to be able to say *'I haven't got time'*, when we dig down a bit deeper there are often other reasons for not getting round to doing tasks:

- ⧗ We feel overwhelmed by a task and don't know where to start

- ⧗ We don't feel confident about starting or completing a task

- ⧗ We feel like we don't have the right skills or resources that are needed to tackle the task

- ⧗ Fear of failure or success

- ⧗ The task is not actually a real priority to us

- ⧗ There aren't any consequences if we don't do the task

You need to be honest with yourself about what's really stopping you. When you identify the real reason for not doing something, then you can start working out how to address the issues. If you are not feeling confident or feel like you don't have the right resources, you can take action to overcome that. If something isn't one of your priorities, do you need to do it? Or do you simply feel obligated to do so? For example, I had a client who said she didn't do things because she was lazy. She didn't come across as being lazy so we dug a little deeper and the real problem was that she was fearful of being rejected.

Saying '*I haven't got time*' almost gives away your power. Being honest about why you are not doing something puts you back in control and is more empowering. Feel the difference between '*I haven't got time to cook from scratch*' and '*I'd rather do something else than spend time cooking from scratch*'. This can also be a helpful way of handling situations where others are asking you to do things. For example, your neighbour asks if you'd like to join the local group to organise the Christmas fayre. If you say you haven't got time, it leaves room for the other person to try and suggest solutions such as '*But it will only take an hour a week, what if you could just join us on Tuesday evenings?* So rather than making an excuse and saying you haven't got time, be honest and say something along the lines of '*Thanks for asking me. I have other things that I need to focus on right now so it's not something I can commit to.*'

When you say yes to something that you don't want to do, it can lead to various consequences. You may feel resentful, it could mean you have to give up other things that are important to you or you are not able to do the job as well as you would like because you are having to squeeze it in. Nobody wins in this situation.

Saying no to things is a crucial tool in your time-management tool box. When you start saying no to things that are not your priority, it leaves room for the things that **are** important.

Do it or ditch it?

So, how do you know whether you should be saying yes, no, or just getting on with it? Some things in life we have to do, regardless of whether we like it or not. Bills have to be paid, we need to keep up with cleaning if we don't want to live in squalor, we have to eat; these basic activities take up time but are vital to keeping us alive and well. There are ways of making these tasks more efficient such as setting up direct debits or standing orders, or getting someone in to do the cleaning, and eating ready meals. Not all of these solutions will suit us but it is worth remembering that we always have options; sometimes just knowing that helps us to feel more in control.

In the last chapter we identified the things that are important to us, so these should be our priorities and treated that way. This can help us decide whether to do something or ditch it. Perhaps it is time to accept that something isn't our priority and let it go. If it remains on our 'to do' list, literally or mentally, it's going to be taking up our precious energy.

When I used to note down my New Year's resolutions, I would often write 'run a marathon'. It felt like something good to aim for. However, although I enjoy my jogging, I'm not what you would call a 'serious' runner and it wasn't really that important to me, so there was no point in it being on my list in the first place. Keeping fit and being healthy is important to me so now I ensure that staying active is a regular part of my routine without feeling like I need to run a marathon.

If there is a task on your to do list (whether that's in your head or written down somewhere) and it keeps getting pushed back from one week to the next, it's probably time to ask yourself if it definitely needs to be tackled. If it does, set a time and date to do it and get on with it. If it doesn't, accept that it is not important and delete it from your list. This frees up mental space immediately and you will feel better; nobody needs to be carrying extra baggage around!

If you have lots of things to do and you are feeling overwhelmed, there is a simple exercise that can help you decide what needs doing, what can be discarded and the order in which to do them.

Write down your 'to do' list, then look at the matrix below (you can download a copy of this from *senseofdirection.life/book-resources*).

Importance / Urgency matrix

	Urgent	Not urgent
Important	**Do now!**	Do later / Schedule
Not important	Delegate	Discard

Now work out in which box each item on your 'to do' list needs to go. Add items or things that are both urgent and important, with severe consequences if not done, in the *Do now* box. Items that are important but not urgent go in the *Do later / schedule* box. Things that are urgent but not important to you can be delegated where possible. Finally, ask yourself if those tasks that are neither urgent nor important can be discarded. Once you have identified the different categories for each task, you can then plan the order in which to do them or how to tackle them.

Sometimes just going through an exercise like this will help you differentiate the tasks and see what **really** needs doing. If there are still many items that you feel you need to '*do now*' then it's time to review your commitments. Perhaps you need to speak to other people about what is realistic if a task relates to them (e.g. you said you would do something for them) or get other people on board to help you. For example, if you live in a household with other people, are they doing their share of the housework? Even children can help with tidying up, especially if you make it into a game.

> '*For all of life's disparities in talent and wealth, each of us is given exactly the same amount of time in each hour, and in each day and in each year. It is a limited amount, and it is impossible for anyone to be so rich in 'time' that he can enjoy every single one of the things which time may buy.... There are choices to be made.*'
> – William Rehnquist, former US chief justice

What do you want and when by?

The key to better time management is being intentional about how you use your time. Look back at your priorities from the last chapter and your time log then answer these questions in your notebook:

⧖   What would you like to be doing more of?

⏳   What's stopping you from doing more?

⏳   What would you like to be doing less of?

⏳   What's stopping you from doing less?

By taking time to review and then being intentional about what you truly want, you can start to use your time more effectively. When you have something that you would like to achieve, it's useful to set a goal or an intention to make it happen. It's important that your head and heart are in alignment when you create this goal, otherwise you will struggle to accomplish it. It can be helpful to add a timeframe so you know when you are going to do what. An example of a goal might to be run the London Marathon or get a promotion at work. These are distinct aims that you can work towards. A wish is something that you would like but haven't given any real thought or energy to. This might include *'I wish I was rich,'* but then not taking any action.

It doesn't matter if it takes a couple of years to get there, the sooner you start, the sooner you will achieve it. If it is a long-term goal it is worth dividing it up into smaller steps and identifying marker posts along the way. Perhaps your goal is to buy your own house. You know this is going to take a few years to reach, so break it down into key milestones such as saving 'x' amount for a deposit, getting mortgage quotes, identifying the area you want to live in, viewing houses and so on. And then you can break down each of these milestones into yet smaller steps, each with their own timescale. So for example, the saving a deposit milestone could include steps such as reviewing your budget, saving 'x' each month and reducing your spending. Some of these steps are discrete, one time tasks, whereas others are ongoing; but whichever they are, you need to identify when you are going to do them or just start! You can monitor your progress and adjust timescales or actions as you go along.

Being intentional about how you use your time allows you to set more realistic time frames for planning and creating space for the things that matter to you. This could be something simple such as starting a new hobby.

Fitting it all in

Most of us would look at our week and say we haven't got time for anything extra but then one morning, your washing machine breaks and floods the kitchen or you fall over and break your arm. Suddenly, your priorities have to change, so you find time to sit in A & E for three hours (if you are lucky!) or mop up the mess in your kitchen and find a plumber. Often, time management is a matter of perspective. The examples listed above are unpleasant to deal with and occur out of the blue. But what if you were a little more intentional about making time for the fun things and activities that are important to you?

There are various time management tools and techniques out there; it's often the case of trying different ones to suit you and your circumstances. I've tried many over the years and now use a combination of them depending on the type of activity I'm doing. I'll share a few of them here.

1. Scheduling

Sometimes we put pressure on ourselves, feeling like we must get everything done right now! Frequently, we can do everything, but not all at once. This is where scheduling comes in. If you want to ensure things happen, you have to set aside time to do them. For me, scheduling doesn't have to be completely rigid, but my time needs to have some structure. The key is to start with your important elements and add them into your schedule first then continue adding the other tasks around them. There is a wonderful visual analogy for this using a jar and various contents (search *Jar of Life* on YouTube or see p. 147 for more information). The main idea is a powerful demonstration of these elements:

Seeds: small trivial aspects of life that can be lovely to have (or the small stuff that irritates us!)

Pebbles: money, house, car etc. – important, but material possessions

Golf balls: health, family, friends, passions etc. – the important things that make life worthwhile.

Depending on which order you put them into the jar, determines whether they all fit in. If you put the seeds and pebbles in first, then only a couple of the golf balls will likely fit on top. Whereas if you do it the other way round, all the golf balls can fit in and the seeds and pebbles will fill the gaps. If you can't fit all the seeds in, it doesn't matter, as the important stuff is taken care of.

At the start of each week I look at my diary and task list. This includes the goals I'm working on, the set appointments I have and any household chores that need doing. I then create a schedule that I print out and put up in my kitchen. I used to write specific times for everything but I found I couldn't always stick to them and then it would become useless and I would be demoralised. I now write times for set appointments or coaching calls and then allocate a part of the day to other tasks that I want to get done. For example, I've already mentioned that being healthy and active is important to me so that gets scheduled first thing in a morning, unless I know for definite that I will be doing something active later in the day. I've learned over the years that generally, if I don't exercise first thing in the morning there is no guarantee that I'll do it later on.

When you are intentional about getting the right activities in your schedule on a daily basis, it will naturally lead to forming helpful habits that serve you long term.

2. MITs (Most Important Tasks)

Another technique that can help is identifying your MITs. Choose one or two (at a push, three) tasks that need to be tackled that day and do those first, before you do anything else. That way you'll have cleared the most important things and anything else you get done is a bonus.

3. Timer

If you work full time or have lots of responsibilities it can feel overwhelming to squeeze everything in, so this is where you have to be selective and use your time wisely. I would advise that you set boundaries around when you do something and for how long. When you are doing activities such as scrolling through social media, which can eat time up, it's worth deciding how long you want to allocate to it, then set a timer and stick to it. Parkinson's Law states that work expands to fill the time allotted; so for example, if you give yourself 3 hours to complete your accounts or sort out your bills, it will take you 3 hours. However, if you only allocate 1.5 hours, you would still probably get it all done.

Along the same lines is the Pomodoro Technique. This involves setting a timer for 25 minutes and focusing on one task only, then having a 5 minute break where you get up and move your attention. You then repeat this a couple more times, having a longer break (20 – 30 minutes) after 3 to 4 rounds of focused attention. If 25 minutes feels like a stretch, just do 10 to 15 minutes of something – you will be surprised at how much you can do in that time!

4. Taking breaks

Notice how breaks are built into the Pomodoro Technique. I regularly hear people say, *'I haven't got time for a lunch break!'* but this is illusory; you probably haven't got time to NOT take a break. Taking regular breaks helps us to be more productive and focused as we are more likely to come back to the task feeling refreshed. Just because you are sitting at your desk or computer for hours on end does not mean you are being productive for that length of time; there is a difference between being busy and being productive. When I start to feel my attention wavering or I start procrastinating, I get up and go for a short walk. This shifts my energy and gives me some space to think about what I'm doing, so I can refocus my attention.

Taking longer breaks and having holidays is also important. Being able to switch off completely from regular routines can be a very helpful way to re-energise and reset. Use your out-of-office function to manage expectations and let people know when you'll be able to respond (then avoid the temptation of checking and dealing with emails while you're away!). I have a rule where I don't go on any social media on Sundays; I call it 'social media free Sunday'!

5. Eat That Frog!

Brian Tracy's book, *Eat That Frog!* has numerous suggestions for managing your time effectively. The main premise of the book is identifying your 'frog' (hardest, ugliest task) and 'eating' (completing) that task first. The idea behind this is once we've tackled the hardest task, it's easier to concentrate on other things that need doing. Have you ever put off an important phone call? You know you have to make this call but you keep doing other things first. However, the call is still taking up your attention as you are thinking about it (or trying not to think about it!) until you bite the bullet and actually make the call. I have heard arguments for and against this technique; some people believe that starting with a slightly easier task, rather than the hardest, is better for building motivation. It's worth experimenting with what works for you.

6. Doubling up

Some activities can be done in parallel. For example, listening to audio books or podcasts while doing household chores or travelling. This not only helps you to use your time more efficiently but can also make the other activity more enjoyable. We can even use the pockets of time when we are waiting for appointments or waiting in telephone queues, especially if you have to do this regularly. It is about being organised and planning ahead.

I often used to struggle with getting somewhere on time because I would always squeeze in one more thing before I set off. I used to see time waiting as time wasted; however, I learned to reframe this thinking. Arriving a few minutes early, means I am less stressed rather than feeling flustered walking in late. If I am more than a few minutes early, I can use the time to message friends or simply enjoy having breathing space in my day.

If we are naturally busy people, it is easy to get swept along in 'doing' mode all the time. There is always something vying for our attention or some task waiting to be completed. But, it is worth remembering that we are human beings not human 'doings'! Simply being present and enjoying the moment is a worthwhile use of our time, whether we are alone or with others.

We can either find stillness in a physical sense or a mindful way. For example, when I go out walking I may be physically moving but it gives my mind an opportunity to be calmer and less distracted. I find this sort of activity is a good use of my time, as I often have my best ideas whilst walking or can untangle some concerns; it is great for my well-being in general.

> *'Between our minds and our legs, one of them is going to wander. Sit still and our minds want to ramble. Get up and start walking, and our minds can slow down and be more focused'*
> *– Arianna Huffington, Greek-American author and businesswoman*

Time is precious; it is not about how much you can fit in one day but fitting in the right things. If we don't use our time wisely we can end up exhausted, feeling as if we're always missing out and wondering why we're not enjoying life.

————————— Checklist —————————

⊕   Record your activities for 2–3 days (using the time log template) and notice how you currently spend your time

⊕   Use the Importance / Urgency grid to prioritise your 'to do' list

⊕   Consider what you would like to make more time for and how you could do that

⊕   Identify your time wasters or things you would like to do less of, then take steps to make it happen

⊕   Watch the *Jar of Life* video

⊕   Experiment with the different time management tools and see which works best for you or for different activities

CHAPTER SIX

H for Health

'The groundwork of all happiness is health'
– Leigh Hunt, English critic and essayist

Health is another huge topic that could fill an entire book so I will just be covering some key themes that influence our life rhythm. As the saying goes, '*Your Health is Your Wealth*', without good health, life becomes more challenging.

Health impacts so many different aspects of our life, affecting our overall well-being. Good health is not just the absence of disease and injury; it is about feeling good and functioning well. When we start to consciously look after our health we can then notice a difference in how we approach life. When we feel healthy we generally have higher levels of resilience and can tackle challenges more easily.

Core principle: Identify what good health means to you and how to maintain it.

In this chapter, we'll take a look at different aspects of health, consider what good health means to us as an individual and start to identify when we're going off track. I'll share some tips for maintaining and improving your health and differentiate between self-care and self-comfort.

So, what are the different aspects of health? There are various ways to label them but I tend to think of four main categories: physical, mental, emotional and financial health. These all play a big role in how we experience life and are often intertwined.

Physical health

As I mentioned above, health is not just the absence of illness and disease. Some people have long-term medical conditions or physical disabilities and still feel healthy. Physical health is influenced by how we nourish our bodies, the level of physical activity we engage in and how fit we are.

Beyond a clinical definition, health is very individual and means different things to different people. Sometimes we can gradually get worn down by stress, life circumstances or physical ailments and forget what it's like to have good health. So, let's think about what good health means to you on an individual level.

Try this: Make a list in your notebook of activities or behaviours you are able to undertake when you have good health and how you feel in your body.

Reflecting and writing things down helps to bring them to our conscious awareness. This can help to remind us of what we are capable of when we look after ourselves and give us a nudge to refocus on our health. If you've been struggling with your physical health recently, perhaps place this list somewhere prominent as a visual reminder to make healthy choices if appropriate.

When we are feeling stressed or busy, we can end up neglecting our bodies and health. We may feel we haven't got time to exercise (if you still feel this way, read the previous chapter again!) and grab unhealthy snacks as we rush from one thing to another. Or, our life circumstances may change, resulting in different habits. For a while, I had a job which involved lots of driving and attending events with delicious food. A year later, when I had to attend the GP surgery for a regular appointment, the nurse weighed me and I was devastated about the amount of weight I'd put on. Obviously, it made complete sense when I thought about it; I'd spent most of my time either sitting at a computer or driving, I'd let my eating habits slide and I hadn't compensated by being more active. Recognising I'd put on weight was the nudge I needed to reset my healthy habits.

Try this: What are the indicators that your physical health is going off track? What habits start to slide or creep in?

Recognising when we are going off track is important as it allows us to do something about it sooner rather than later. Becoming aware of your habits and symptoms, such as clothes feeling a little tighter, getting out of breath more easily, snacking on junk food or skin not looking as clear, can all be reminders that you are not looking after yourself and provide the prompt to reset. It can also address any underlying reasons why you are not looking after yourself as well as you could be. Are you feeling overwhelmed? Have your circumstances changed?

It's important to remember there is a time lag between our actions and their consequences. That might be a few days, a few weeks or even a few months. Sometimes we might think we're getting away with eating a bit more but then the scales tell us a different story a couple of weeks later. If we were to put on weight straight after eating a chocolate bar, or developed diabetes after eating a bag of sweets or experienced heart disease after smoking one cigarette, then we'd probably make different choices. Similarly, there is a time lag between our healthy habits and seeing the benefits. We don't suddenly grow our muscles after one trip to the gym or lose weight because we've eaten better that day. It's a series of habits and behaviours over a period of time that leads to results.

As we age, our physical health naturally changes but that's not an excuse for not staying active and looking after ourselves. In fact, if we look after ourselves physically then it helps to mitigate the ageing process. My parents are both still very active; swimming, dancing three times a week and walking daily. My dad is in his seventies and still goes running a few times a week too. My grandad was a very active man, playing golf, tenpin bowling and going on his exercise bike, right into his nineties. Losing muscle strength is one of the main factors that impacts on our physical health as we age, so where possible, it's vital that we keep using our muscles.

It's important to take heed of any persistent physical ailments that present themselves as they can be the body's way of making us take notice and take action. Sometimes when we've had a really busy period we end up getting a heavy cold or some other bug; I see this as the body's way of telling us to take a rest and slow down. We often know that we should be taking better care of ourselves but don't, so the body has to take action and force us to take stock. We have to make time for our health otherwise we are forced to make time for our illness. I encourage you not to get to this point!

Improving physical health

You may have noticed that I've used the term 'physical activity' rather than 'exercise'. To stay fit and healthy you don't have to go to the gym or take part in team sports. Gardening, DIY, housework and dancing are all physically active. Anything that gets your heart pumping faster, makes you feel warmer or gets your muscles working, is going to help. The key to increasing your physical activity level is to do something that you enjoy. Look for different classes in your community or think outside the box and try new things. You can also make the mundane more enjoyable by tweaking them, for example, putting on your favourite tunes while you do the housework. Getting a friend or family member to join your activities can be helpful – it is not only more sociable but you then have some accountability too.

Try this: Consider what steps you can take **now** to improve your physical health.

How can you increase the amount of physical activity you do? It could be as simple as parking your car further away from your destination, getting off the bus a stop earlier or using the stairs instead of the lift. Fitting in active breaks during your day is an easy way to increase your level of movement. This could include doing some star jumps while you're waiting for the kettle to boil, walking over to speak to a colleague rather than emailing them, going upstairs to the loo or taking a short brisk walk at lunch time. Little changes and tweaks to our behaviours all add up and can make a big difference. When we make being active part of our day it becomes a habit and not something that we have to specifically make time for. Engaging in physical activity has a positive influence on our mental health too.

Mental Health

Mental health affects how we think, feel and behave. It influences our ability to handle stress, how we interact with others and the world around us. Mental health seems to be a buzz phrase and high on the agenda in numerous arenas at the moment; I think this is because people are now finally realising how important and pervasive mental health is. When we hear the term 'mental health' it is often in the context of poor or lack of mental health. Perhaps it's one of those things that we don't appreciate until we are struggling. When we have poor mental health, it usually affects everything – our ability to work, our relationships and our physical health.

Poor mental health can be due to underlying physical deficiencies or genetics, but it's often linked to our circumstances or the amount and type of stress we are experiencing. It is worth noting that some stress is good for us as it provides stimulation and motivation. However, if we experience prolonged or excessive stress it can have an adverse effect on us. By becoming more self-aware and recognising some of the signs that our mental health is deteriorating, it gives us the opportunity to take action, stop that decline and put things in place to improve our situation.

Try this: Take some time to reflect on what signs you notice when you are feeling stressed or your mental health is declining. For example, perhaps the quality of your sleep changes, you start to bite your nails, you withdraw from family and friends, or your appetite changes.

Rather than ignoring these signs and symptoms, it's important to address them as soon as you can. If we let things slide too far it can be an uphill struggle to make things better again. Try to identify what's led to the decline; is it a particular situation? Not taking care of yourself? Feeling overwhelmed? Relationship issues?

Actions accumulate and create a compound effect. If you've had a couple of late nights, been super busy at work and not done any physical activity for a week or so, these actions are going to lead to negative outcomes. By identifying the triggers and unhelpful behaviours it can enable us to find the right solution to improve things. Sometimes just recognising what we have and haven't got control over can support us in directing our energy appropriately.

Try this: Circle of Control. Draw a large circle in your notebook. On the inside of the circle write down all the things in your life that you can control (e.g. what you eat, what you wear, how you spend your time). On the outside, write down all the things you can't control that are bothering you (e.g. the weather, politics, other people's behaviour).

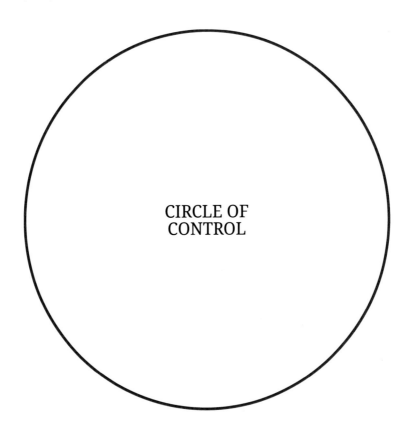

CIRCLE OF
CONTROL

Now there are a few steps you can take:

- Focus the majority of your energy on the things you can control.

- Accept that there are things you can't control and let them go.

- Consider how you can respond to or influence the things you can't control. For example, although you can't control the weather, you could buy some good waterproofs and make going out in the rain more comfortable. Although you can't change politics, if it's something you are passionate about you could get involved with your local council.

Improving mental health

It is vital to recognise what good mental health means to us. Becoming more self-aware helps us to understand ourselves on a deeper level and make better choices. We have a responsibility for looking after ourselves and ensuring we engage in behaviours and make decisions that are going to enhance our health. People often blame external factors for their poor mental well-being; that certainly contributes to it but there is much more in our control than we give ourselves credit for as hopefully you've realised from the *Circle of Control* activity above. It is not only what happens to you that's important but how you **respond** to what happens. This is something we will look at further in the chapter on mindset.

Try this: Take a few minutes to consider what good mental health means to you. Jot a few ideas down in your notebook. How do you feel when you are at your best, when you have good mental health? How do you interact with other people? What habits and behaviours do you display?

This can be a useful exercise to remind you what you are like when you are in good mental health and what benefits you gain when you look after yourself. Once again, it's the little factors that contribute to your mental health such as:

- Getting good quality sleep

- Taking time out to do fun / leisure activities

- Allowing time for rest

- Getting fresh air and natural daylight

- Spending time in nature

- Spending time with people who inspire or uplift you

- Eating nourishing food

Time spent looking after your mental health will pay dividends in the long run. You will be able to cope with life's challenges more easily and simply enjoy life to a greater extent.

Emotional Health

Emotional health is linked to mental health in some respects but is subtly different. It's about how we think, feel and express our emotions. Take a look back at chapter two on relationships where I describe emotions as messengers. As human beings, we get the privilege of experiencing a whole spectrum of emotions; some of them are more pleasant than others, but none of them are 'bad' as such. Being able to identify and label the different emotions we are feeling can help us to manage them more effectively. Take a look at the Emotion Wheel again.

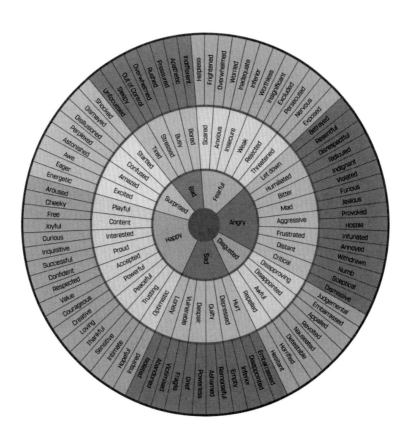

It's natural that we experience different emotions; we aren't going to feel positive 100% of the time. Emotions often arise in response to external circumstances. For example, if we lose someone close to us, it is natural to feel grief, loss or despair. If we start a new relationship or do something fun, then we'll feel excitement and joy. Emotions are part of the experience, and we should never try to repress them, as this can create problems in future.

However, it's important that we express them in a healthy way, especially those we might label as more negative. If we are feeling angry, then doing something physical can help to discharge the energy safely. This could be exercising, sports, dancing or creative / artistic activities. Creative activities can be a satisfying way to express emotions (especially when you struggle to find the right words), as you get the benefit from both the physical act of creating and the visual result of the finished article. It doesn't matter whether you are 'arty' or not; it's not about creating a masterpiece but something that is personal and individual to you. Creative activities form one key part of my JOY Day Retreats, as it's a lovely way to practise self-care and explore different aspects of wellbeing.

Sometimes, we may feel embarrassed about crying but there is nothing wrong with doing so – it is another way of releasing emotion. If someone is crying, don't tell them to stop and don't get embarrassed; just be with them and make them feel it's safe to cry in front of you. If you are supporting other people who are experiencing difficult emotions, be mindful of your own well-being and try not to absorb too much of their energy or feelings. You may need to limit the time spent with them or ensure you do activities that lift your own spirit after being with them.

Emotions can also arise in response to our thoughts. Recalling fond memories can make us smile, whereas if we are worried about a forthcoming interview we may feel anxious. This is a reminder that our mind is incredibly powerful and if we can learn to harness it more for our benefit, rather than being a slave to it, then we'll get along in life far more easily.

If you start to feel sad or worried without a specific external trigger, consider what you are thinking about. Was it something that happened or something that you are anticipating? Either way, consider if there is anything you can do to change it or if you wish to pursue the thoughts further.

Try this: *Thought switching* is a technique where you actively choose to switch the focus of your thoughts. The key to this is being consciously aware of what you are thinking about in the first place and making the decision that you no longer wish to think about it. It's a technique that takes practise but really does work.

If I find myself ruminating on something that's not helpful or unpleasant then I'll literally say 'STOP', either in my head or out loud and then consciously choose to think about something else.

'The greatest weapon against stress is our ability to choose one thought over another'
– William James, American philosopher & psychologist

Mindfulness for emotional health

Mindfulness is becoming more popular as a way to improve our well-being, and for good reason. There have been many proven benefits to practising mindfulness and it can be very simple. In this often tremendously busy world, we can be distracted by many things and conduct ourselves on autopilot. Mindfulness is a technique in which we become present in the moment. It's about learning to become consciously aware of ourselves and the world around us. We pay attention to how we feel and what we are actually doing, which can help us make better choices that are in alignment with what we genuinely want.

In addition to the STOP technique that I introduced in the Relationships chapter, there is another mindfulness tool called RAIN that can help us to deal with our emotions.

> R = **Recognise** that you are experiencing a particular emotion
> A = **Acknowledge** what the emotion is, label it
> I = **Investigate** your body – what's going on, thoughts, sensations and how you are feeling
> N = **Non-identify.** Is this who I am or just an experience, e.g. *'I am* **feeling** *angry'* rather than *'I* **am** *angry'.*

You can then consciously choose how you wish to proceed and whether you want to change your thoughts. This exercise, as with any mindfulness technique, takes practise. It is worth setting an intention to learn and persevere as you'll reap the rewards by being able to deal with situations more calmly and not getting knocked off balance when a trigger comes along. I suggest you start off with small, less significant experiences first to hone your skills, so that when something bigger arises, you can rely on the exercise with more confidence.

Financial Health

I'm not an expert in financial matters so I won't go into much detail around this area but I do encourage you to look at your financial situation and consider your relationship with money. Finances and money are often a big source of stress for people, especially with the rising cost of living. If money worries play on your mind and you struggle with budgeting, then I recommend getting some help. There are many charities and organisations (as well as courses) that can help you. *Money Helper* (*moneyhelper.org.uk*) is a great place to start for practical advice on all financial matters. If you have issues such as feeling uncomfortable about investing in yourself or asking for money in return for your services, then there are coaches who specialise in this area. In addition, *Secrets of the Millionaire Mind,* by T. Harv Ecker, provides help to improve your money mindset. When your finances are under control (regardless of how much or how little money you have), and you are comfortable with money, you often have greater peace of mind.

Self-care and self-comfort

In the Habits chapter, I introduced the idea of self-care and self-comfort. I'd like to expand further on these ideas here as they also relate to our health. Some people may think of self-care as rather 'navel-gazing' but actually, it's the opposite. As well-functioning adults we should be practising self-care and taking responsibility for our own well-being, rather than relying on others to make us feel better. Our choices and actions lead to consequences and results; when we fully understand that and take responsibility for those actions, we become empowered to make different choices.

Self-care is about looking after ourselves by putting in place supportive habits that are ongoing, such as ensuring we have time to rest and do the fun things in life. If we don't give and 'allow' ourselves this time, then we are likely to burn out or at the very least, feel miserable, which benefits no one!

Remember: Self-care is NOT selfish

I have talked about self-comfort as activities that provide short-term benefits, such as eating chocolate when we feel stressed. However, I now want to look at self-comfort from a slightly different angle and a deeper level. When you are experiencing an uncomfortable emotion it is incredibly helpful to practise one of the mindfulness techniques I've mentioned above and sit with the emotion for a short while. Tune into what you are feeling and thinking and then ask yourself, *'What would really help to comfort me at this time?'* Maybe it's doing something creative, listening to music, getting out in nature, reaching out to a friend or seeking professional support. This helps us take control of our well-being rather than placing it in the care of others. This is not to say that you shouldn't ask for help from others; seeking support from appropriate others is important, but it's also about doing your part. For example, if you want to lose weight and join a slimming club but then continue to make unhealthy food choices, you can't blame anyone else for your lack of progress.

I don't want to sound harsh here! I'm simply encouraging you to take a deeper look at your behaviours and habits, as this is where the power lies. We can't change anyone else, only ourselves, and therefore need to choose wisely about where we invest our energy.

> *'When at work, work. When at play, play.'*
> – Jim Rohn, American author and entrepreneur

Energy

Besides time, energy is also one of our most precious assets. We only have so much energy available to us in a day and that can depend on a number of factors, such as the amount of fuel our body has in terms of the food we eat, but also mental energy and how we are feeling. If we don't eat the right sort or amount of food then it leaves us feeling weak or sluggish, which is why nourishing ourselves with a good quality diet is vital to our well-being. The type of food we eat can also affect our mood.

Try this: Keep a food journal in your notebook for a few days and take notice of your energy levels and mood. How do you feel after eating certain foods? How does your energy level change during the day? Do you notice any patterns when you eat certain types of food?

In terms of mental energy, we may associate this with how motivated we feel to do certain tasks. This can be linked to our sense of purpose or our 'why' for doing things. The greater the degree of purpose, the more energy we are likely to find to accomplish whatever it is. Mental energy can be used up by challenging circumstances, when we are trying to process difficult emotions or solve a problem. We also use up mental energy when worrying, which is why it's important to be mindful of our thoughts.

'Worrying is like a rocking chair,
it gives you something to do but gets you nowhere'
–Anon

There are many different facets to our health and it is a key part of living our best life. Hopefully now you can see how all the elements of RHYTHM are intertwined and impact on one another. We have one final element to explore that pulls everything together, and that's our mindset.

─────────────── Checklist ───────────────

◉   Make a list of things you can do or already
    do when you feel physically good

◉   List the signs that your physical health is
    going off track

◉   Choose one or two steps that you can
    implement to start improving your physical
    health

◉   Complete the *Circle of Control* exercise

◉   Jot down what good mental health means to
    you

◉   Practise the RAIN exercise

◉   Do a financial audit – what's your
    relationship with money like? Are there
    areas you want to improve?

◉   Keep a food diary for a few days and notice
    the impact of different foods on your
    energy levels and mood

CHAPTER SEVEN

M for Mindset

'Don't limit yourself.
Many people limit themselves to what they think
they can do.
You can go as far as your mind lets you.
What you believe, remember, you can achieve.'
– Mary Kay Ash, Founder of Mary Kay Cosmetics

Mindset is a huge topic and potentially life changing, so this is a great element to end on. If you implement the ideas and exercises in this chapter it will literally transform your life. I find this topic fascinating and love learning about it. Life is a huge learning opportunity and our mindset makes the difference as to how we experience it. There will always be challenges and how we respond to them will depend on our mindset. Having the right mindset helps to smooth out the extremes and gives us different perspectives on situations so that we don't get sucked into life's dramas so easily.

Core principle: Develop a mindset for success and confidently deal with life's challenges

The first question I'd like to ask you is this: Do you believe that you live in a generally friendly universe or a mainly unfriendly universe? Trusting that the world is out to support you will influence how you interact with the people around you and how you see situations unfolding, whilst also enabling you to enjoy life to a greater degree. If this isn't already how you view the world, I encourage you to start working on changing this; you will see why and how this is so important below.

In this chapter we'll take a look at growth and fixed mindsets, feedback, failure, overcoming obstacles, the power of language and gratitude. There is much to cover so let's get started.

Growth or Fixed?

One way mindset is often classified is either growth or fixed. People with a fixed mindset generally believe they are born with a particular skill set or not; that our abilities are innate. So for example, they are either a natural leader or not. However, due to this belief, if someone doesn't pick up a new skill straight away they tend to give up quite easily as they believe they don't have the ability and won't get any better at it. You might say *I'm just not good with numbers*. This is a limiting belief and one that will hinder your progress because you are less likely to commit to practising and therefore limit your opportunity for improvement, because if you don't believe you have a skill and can't develop it why would you keep practising?

On the other hand, a growth mindset gives us an advantage because we believe that we can develop and learn a skill set with effort. This sort of belief and attitude will encourage us to practise and look for ways to improve. We won't give up very easily and we're more likely to try different ways of doing things. We are more open to feedback that will help us look for solutions.

There are many ways to cultivate a growth mindset:

- Believe you can change and improve

- Keep an open mind and look for alternative ways of doing things

- Don't fear failure

- Value and reward effort

- Actively seek feedback

- Practise and review

As you can see, feedback is important to helping us develop but it is something that people sometimes fear because it often feels negative. To overcome this, read on...

Giving & Receiving Feedback

Feedback can help us to learn, improve, grow and understand how our actions affect other people. It can also help to confirm our strengths and what we do well. Feedback should be constructive and informational, and not simply negative comments. There will be times when we are receiving feedback and there may be times when we are the one giving it.

Feedback can be informal, such as passing comments from people or how we interpret our experiences. It can also be formal, such as a one-to-one at work, questionnaires and so on.

Tips for **giving** feedback

- Consider if it is an appropriate time and place, especially if it is formal feedback

- Give feedback in person where possible

- Be prepared and consider what you want from the discussion and what your key points are

- Concentrate on the behaviour rather than the person (name the behaviour, how you feel about it and what you want)

- Balance the content – it shouldn't be all critical

- Be specific, using examples where possible, and realistic

- Own the feedback using 'I statements' e.g. *I feel x when you do y*

- Be timely – don't bottle it up

- Offer continuing support and suggestions for improvements where appropriate

Tips for **receiving** feedback

- Listen without interrupting

- Be aware of your responses such as your body language, tone of voice and emotions

- Take time out and come back to the discussion if needs be

- Be open minded and see it as an opportunity for learning or growth

- Avoid getting defensive or justifying

- Recognise triggers (use the RAIN technique from earlier)

- Don't take it personally

- Adopt a growth mindset

- Exercise self-compassion

- Understand what's been said by seeking clarification or asking questions where necessary

- Reflect and decide on a course of action

- Follow up where appropriate

Regardless of whether you are giving or receiving the feedback, thank the person and recognise that it may have been uncomfortable or challenging. We often learn more when things don't go to plan, so never worry about things being a 'failure'.

Feedback not failure

The following acronym for fail can be a source of encouragement:

First **A**ttempt **I**n **L**earning.

It reminds us that learning and failure go together. Often in our society there is a negative feeling towards failing and therefore it is common that people fear failure. However, it is natural that we won't always 'get' something first time and things may not go to plan, but that doesn't mean you're a failure. There is a big difference between something failing and being a failure. In general I don't like the term failure and try to avoid using it. Feedback is a more accurate description; take the famous quote by Thomas Edison when he was describing his journey with inventing the light bulb:

'I've not failed. I've just found 10,000 ways that won't work'

There are hundreds of examples of items that we would not have if people gave up when they were inventing them! By starting to believe that we can't fail, we then have a very different attitude towards trying something in the first place. Think how empowering this mindset could be! This is not to say that it is easy or comfortable when things don't go to plan, but it is most certainly not wasted energy or time.

A little note on life lessons and feedback from the universe (by this, I mean something bigger than ourselves that is perhaps trying to guide us). I believe that we will keep encountering the same issues until we've learnt the lesson we are meant to learn. For example, we swap jobs but get frustrated when we end up experiencing the same problems. Or we notice the same patterns occurring in our relationships; different person but the same outcome. This is life's way of telling us we need to do some inner work and take a look at ourselves, our behaviours and our beliefs. This can be done via reading, attending courses or getting professional help from a coach or therapist.

Overcoming obstacles

There will **always** be challenges in life that can make things difficult. However, by changing our perspective, we can choose to see these challenges as stepping stones rather than obstacles. Ask yourself whether the challenge is truly an obstacle, or are you simply finding an excuse to not do something? Perhaps anxiety is stopping you or fear of failure? Or the challenge is not high on your list of priorities. Sometimes we may even unconsciously self-sabotage our success. This might present as not following through on actions, slow timing decisions or finding fault where there is none. Is this something you do?

Self-sabotaging or finding obstacles could also be linked to our beliefs, or more accurately, our limiting beliefs. We may not be consciously aware of these but they can influence our behaviour. Go back and revisit the chapter on Relationships to remind yourself of how some of your beliefs may be hindering your progress. Check in with yourself and see what the real barriers are.

If there is genuinely an obstacle, consider what makes it an obstacle – what is the specific problem? Lack of time, not having someone to look after the children, difficulty travelling to somewhere or not enough knowledge? Once you've identified the actual problem then you can start coming up with possible solutions. It's a good time to remind yourself of your 'why', your purpose for wanting to achieve the desired outcome. What are the benefits to be gained by working through this challenge? How strongly do you want to achieve this goal? When we have a strong enough 'why', we can find a way to overcome any obstacles.

Giving up

Although it is useful to have the mindset of overcoming obstacles and pushing through challenges, sometimes there are instances when it's appropriate to 'give up' on a course of action. This might include when:

- Something clearly isn't working

- Your priorities change

- A better option becomes apparent

- The cost / effort outweighs the benefits

Giving up can sound very negative and feel like a fail but there are ways to view this differently. In fact, it is probably more accurate to see it as a change of direction. It's pointless to continue because you feel you have put so much time, money or energy into something; why keep wasting more of these resources? For example, you've spent a year at university studying a particular degree, you're not enjoying it much and you've realised it's not for you. Why would you spend another 2 years doing something you don't enjoy and investing more money into it when you could make a different choice?

It's times or circumstances like these when we may be affected by other peoples' opinions. Other people (often well-meaning family or friends) might think you are making the wrong decision by giving up or not making it work. However, it's not their life and they do not have to live with the consequences. Thank them for their concern, listen with an open mind if you trust that they have something valuable to share, take any wisdom you feel is appropriate but leave the rest, and make your own decision.

Start believing you can't make a 'wrong' decision. There will always be benefits and learning opportunities from whatever action you decide to take. The fear often comes from not knowing which path to choose, but if you know you can't make a wrong decision you have nothing to fear! Adjusting our language when describing our experiences can be one way to help us feel more empowered.

> 'The problem is never how to get new innovative thoughts into your mind, but how to get old ones out'
> – Dee Hock, Founder of Visa

The Power of Words

Language is a powerful tool that can support our mindset. Words convey energy and can influence our feelings and beliefs. As already mentioned, I try to avoid the word 'failure' because I don't think it's very helpful. When things don't go to plan or we seem to be having a run of bad luck, we start to ask ourselves, 'Why is this happening to me?' Our brains like finding answers to questions so it will come up with all sorts of reasons why, such as: 'Because I'm not worthy of x, I deserve to fail, I'm just not good enough', and so on. None of these reasons are particularly helpful or inspiring and can make us feel useless and demotivated.

However, if we change just one word in that question, it can make a huge difference. If we ask ourselves, 'Why is this happening **for** me?' It will generate a different set of answers and feelings. It may seem like a very subtle change of question but it will open our mind to other possibilities. Perhaps something better will come along, maybe there is a lesson we can take from the experience. When we're able to look at it from this perspective, we can start to see the experience almost as a gift; it's trying to give us some sort of feedback that will help us in future. We can learn to look for opportunities and see things from another angle. This is a far more empowering stance point that will encourage us to view the situation in a more positive light, rather than feeling like a victim. So although we can't always control what happens to us, we can control how we *respond* to what happens to us.

Again, I recognise that this is not always easy when we experience something that is upsetting or disappointing but I also believe it can give us some comfort. As with everything else, it takes practise.

Although we can't be positive 100% of the time, our language can influence our feelings and thoughts. *'I can't be bothered'* conveys a total lack of motivation and energy, so no wonder we don't feel like doing whatever it is! It's also often a mask for a deeper reason for not doing something. Perhaps we feel anxious, we fear success or it's just not our priority. If this is something you find yourself saying on a regular basis, check in with yourself and explore what's really going on.

We can use our words to help encourage, motivate and energise us. Refer back to the chapter on Relationships when we learned about re-framing. By adding or changing just one or two words we can alter the feeling and energy behind a sentence. Here are a couple of examples to remind you:

- Instead of 'I'm rubbish at being organised' you could swap that to 'I'm finding ways to be more organised.'

- Instead of 'I **have** to cut my lawn,' try 'I **get** to cut my lawn.' Swapping *have to* with *get to*, is a powerful technique as it reminds you to be grateful for your circumstances; not everyone has the same opportunities or circumstances.

- *I appreciate the privilege of getting older*

- *The more I practise on my guitar the better I become*

- *I enjoy learning different ways of doing things*

This is where the power of affirmations comes in.

Affirmations

An affirmation is a statement that we repeatedly say to ourselves. Affirmations are meant to be positive and empowering, but they can be critical and undermining if you have that negative inner voice chattering all the time. That's why it's important to be aware of your self-talk; if you are constantly criticising yourself it's going to have a detrimental effect on how you feel and behave. If your inner voice is generally negative, start to catch yourself in the act of criticising and then reframe the remark. If it's particularly persistent, say something along the lines of *'Thanks for your opinion but that's not useful now.'* You have to retrain your brain so that the negative voice is no longer the default.

As we've already seen, our thoughts and beliefs affect how we behave, so this is where the power lies. If we can change our thoughts and instil some positive beliefs through our words, it encourages us to behave in a more confident way.

Affirmations are generally stated in the present tense as though you are already doing / believing the statement. Focus on what you **want** rather than what you want to **avoid.** For example, rather than *'I am feeling less stressed'* you might say *'I am feeling calm and in control'.* Affirmations are more helpful if they are short so they are easy to recall, as they work best when repeated regularly. Think of affirmations as instant confidence boosters in your pocket! You can use them as often as you wish and wherever you are. You may choose to say them out loud or in your head; every morning and evening or just when you feel you need a reminder. I have a set of affirmations that I read out loud every morning. I will also sometimes create affirmations to help me with specific situations. Here are some examples:

    Today I make decisions with confidence and know that I will experience benefits from whatever happens.

    I am doing my best and that is good enough

    I can help others whilst also practising self-care

    I am getting better at listening to my intuition

Try this: Choose a particular area of your life and have a go at creating your own affirmations using the guidelines above. Jot these down in your notebook.

An attitude of gratitude

Our attitude plays a large role in our mindset and how we see the world. It influences how we express ourselves and our feelings, which in turn influences our interactions with others. Have you ever met someone who you thought had a chip on their shoulder? It's not usually a wholly pleasant experience or one that you would be keen to repeat, compared to chatting with someone who comes across as enjoying life, which is a far more positive experience. Look back at the Drains and Radiators section in the Relationship chapter; are you a drain or a radiator? How often do you genuinely thank someone for their time or for doing something for you? It's a lovely feeling when someone shows their appreciation as we feel valued and recognised for our efforts. A simple 'thank you' goes a long way and it doesn't cost anything. See who you can thank today as you go about your business, taking notice of how you feel and how they respond.

Cultivating an attitude of gratitude is a powerful tool to help improve our mindset. Gratitude is a feeling of appreciation or being grateful in a genuine way. Being grateful helps us to focus on the blessings in our life and what we already have. When we start to recognise what we already have it helps us to feel a sense of abundance rather than a sense of lack. It encourages us to notice the small things in life such as appreciating the weather or someone holding the door open for us. Sometimes if we are having a 'bad' day and everything seems to be going wrong, we can tap into this attitude of gratitude and look for the things going 'right'. Combine it with the mindset of feedback not failure, as above, and suddenly our day doesn't feel so bad after all.

I regularly use the wheel of life exercise in my workshops. After one workshop, I remember a participant had scored 10 in one particular area of his life. This doesn't happen very often so I was interested to hear what made it a 10. He explained that although he wasn't quite where he wanted to be in that area, he was very happy with the progress he was making. This is such a lovely empowering attitude to have; we can be grateful for what we have, even if we are still striving for more. This makes the journey to our goal more satisfying.

Try this: Start writing a daily gratitude journal or list in your notebook. Take a few minutes at the end of your day (or when you need a reminder) and write down at least three things you are grateful for. I want you to feel deeply that sense of appreciation.

When you are writing your list it's more effective when you are specific. For example, rather than simply saying *'I'm grateful for my friends'* you might say *'I'm grateful that Jo invited me for a cuppa'*. When we start to notice these small acts or elements it helps to reinforce how much we already have in our lives. Getting into this routine on a daily basis encourages us to focus on the good things. During our day it's likely that something may have gone wrong or not quite to plan, but there will still be lots of other things that went right too and it's up to us what we choose to focus on. Even on a terrible day there will be things we can be grateful for, such as having running hot water on tap or a roof over our head.

As mentioned, it is also a good habit to get into thanking people. It's not just about good manners and saying thanks but genuinely showing your appreciation for them. It could be a simple *'Thank you for making me a cup of tea'* or maybe you send them a message or card saying *'Thank you for supporting me during this difficult time'*. After one of my team meetings, I realised how much I appreciate all of the members I work with, so I sent them a message of gratitude. People can be quick to complain about things or moan about other people, but don't always share their thanks. Remember how good it feels to know that you are valued and appreciated.

Try this: Make a list of people you are grateful for in your life. If and when it's appropriate, send a note to say thanks or what you appreciate about them.

I often hear people say *'I'll be happy when... I've got more money, I've got more time, I've found a new partner'* etc. The problem with this attitude is that you are constantly delaying your happiness until a specific outcome is reached, often relying on something external. What happens if you don't reach that outcome? What happens if you do reach that outcome and you're still not happy? Why not be happy now? Why wait? You can choose to find happiness now and if or when you reach your desired outcome, then that's a bonus. If you can't find happiness where you are, there is no guarantee you'll find happiness or satisfaction when you reach a particular destination.

Sometimes we have our ideas the wrong way round. For example, sometimes people say, *'When I'm fitter I'll start going to the gym'.* No! You need to start going to the gym to get fitter. We have to put the action in first before we see the change. Revisit the Habits chapter, and re-read the section on the delay between us putting in the work and getting the results we want.

Now we've looked at all the elements of RHYTHM, you should have some practical tools and fresh ideas to build on and live your own best life. The key, however, is how you implement what you've learned, so there is one final chapter where I pull everything together.

——————————— Checklist ———————————

⊗ When things don't go to plan, ask yourself what you can learn from the experience

⊗ When facing a challenge, consider the different options for tackling it

⊗ Mind your language! Swap:

   • 'To me' > 'For me'
   • 'Have to' > 'Get to'

⊗ Choose an area of your life that you would like to improve and create your own powerful affirmation to support you

⊗ Start a daily gratitude list or journal and aim for a minimum of three things each day

⊗ Send a note or message of thanks to someone in your life who you are grateful for and let them know why

CHAPTER EIGHT

Putting it into Practise

It's one thing to read a book and make notes, but the key to living the life you want is to **take action and implement what you've learned.** In this final chapter, I'll give you some ideas about how to put things into practise and how to keep growing using reflection and reviewing exercises. This is also the time to refer back to your RHYTHM wheel to review where you are now. And finally we'll look at how to bring everything together with a couple of example scenarios so you can see how RHYTHM can help you in any situation.

If you've been completing the exercises and jotting things down in your notebook or journal over the course of the book, you should have already noticed some changes to your approach. If you haven't yet finished all the exercises, set aside time to work through them as that's where the magic will happen.

You are now more aware of your behaviours, habits and thoughts. Increased self-awareness gives us the opportunity to be more intentional and conscious of our decisions and choices. However, increased self-awareness alone does not guarantee transformation; you have to translate it into changing your behaviour.

'Knowing and not doing is the same as not knowing'
– Peter Sage, British entrepreneur & human behaviour expert

Reflection and reviewing

Much of our behaviour is learned, which is good news as it means we can learn new ways of doing things and replace old behaviours. Behaviours are habits and as we saw in the Habits chapter, we have to practise to make them stick. However, there is another aspect that can further support your learning which is reflecting and reviewing. If you look back at the Introduction, I encouraged you to use reflection throughout the book to increase your learning; hopefully this is something you are now doing on a regular basis.

As a reminder, reflecting is about creating a pause to consider our thoughts. We can do this before we respond to something or as a tool to help us learn from a situation that has already happened. Reflecting can help to raise our awareness so that we can gain insight about ourselves. We can then be more mindful and intentional about our actions. There are many formal models of reflection but it doesn't have to be anything complicated. A simple model developed by Professor

Gary Rolfe gets us to ask ourselves three questions: *What? So what? Now what?*

You could do this quickly at the end of each day or after a specific event / situation.

What?

- What happened?

- What emotions and feelings did I experience?

- What was good or challenging?

So what?

- So what does this teach me about myself?

- So what does this teach me about my skills and knowledge?

- So what could I have done better?

Now what?

- Now how can I use what I've learned about myself?

- Now what do I do to improve my skills / behaviours?

- Now what could I do differently next time?

Whereas reflecting is more about looking at our thoughts and inner world, reviewing is more focussed on the external factors of a situation or experience. It can help us assess our progress and performance. This is useful to do if you have been working on developing a specific skill or practising new habits. In the Introduction I asked you to complete the RHYTHM wheel; now is a good time to take a look at your wheel again and see how you would score each section.

- Do you feel differently about any of the sections?

- Have your scores changed? If so, what has made you change them?

- What progress have you noticed?

- Are there areas you would still like to develop further? How can you do this?

It can be helpful to choose one or two of the segments that you would like to improve and plan how you are going to do this. The RHYTHM wheel is a great tool for periodically checking in with yourself to monitor your progress and identify any areas that you would like to develop further.

Reviewing can also be useful if you have experienced a change in circumstances, such as having children, starting or ending a relationship, or changing careers, as your priorities may have altered too. Just because you have always done something in a particular way doesn't mean it continues to be the most effective way.

Reflecting and reviewing on a regular basis is a great habit, but avoid the temptation to start over-analysing situations or your actions, otherwise you may end up going round in circles. Stay light-hearted about things and see life as an experiment or adventure. Here are a few examples to demonstrate how RHYTHM could play out in real life scenarios.

Jack – made redundant

Jack finds out that the company he's working for is making cuts and unfortunately, he will be made redundant in 2 months' time. After the initial shock and panic, Jack takes a step back to look at the bigger picture (adopting a positive Mindset). Although the job is OK and pays quite well, it's not something he enjoys and the commute is longer than he would like, which impacts on his family time. He realises that this is a good time to review what he'd like to do in life. Jack brainstorms all the things he enjoys doing, the skills he has, what he's good at and what is important to him, which helps to highlight his values (reviewing Your Purpose). This information guides Jack towards looking for the right type of work and next steps. The redundancy money will give him some breathing space but won't last forever, therefore he knows he also needs to take practical steps to generate an income. Jack starts a new habit whereby a few evenings a week he spends an hour or two getting on with job related tasks such as updating his CV, completing application forms and reaching out to friends and former colleagues (setting up Habits for success by using his Time wisely and tapping into his Relationship skills when speaking to other people).

Jack recognises that this sort of situation can stress him out so he knows the importance of maintaining his self-care practices, such as going to his running club once a week, getting to bed at a reasonable time and doing fun stuff with his wife and children (looking after his Health). Someone at Jack's running club mentions that there is a job vacancy that they think he would be ideal for, so they send him the link. Jack applies and gets selected for interview. On the day of the interview he reminds himself that whatever happens he will be fine and if he's meant to get the job, he will (Mindset of no such thing as failure). This helps him to feel relaxed and be himself so that the interview panellists naturally warm to him and can see how he would be a good fit in their team (Relationship skills).

I'd just like to take a quick detour and tell you about one of my own experiences with a job interview and how my Mindset helped me. I'd been selected for an interview for a full time role within a regional office of Girlguiding; Girlguiding is something that I've been involved with for many years so I felt the job would be one I'd enjoy. On arrival I was given a task to organise a spreadsheet of data into a graphical form. I somehow managed to delete the spreadsheet and had to ask them to give me another copy; even then I still didn't really know what I was doing, so couldn't produce anything useful to take into the next part of the interview.

Integrity is one of my key values so I had to hold my hands up and say that I hadn't been able to complete the task. Luckily I'd been given the interview questions beforehand so I had prepared well for the second part. I walked out of the interview laughing at myself thinking *'Oh well, it's a long commute which I wouldn't want to do every day – maybe it's not for me, as I really wouldn't want to spend my days working with spreadsheets.'*

So imagine my surprise a few days later when they phoned and offered me the job! However, because of my feelings around the commute and spreadsheets I declined but said that I was still interested in the project they were running if there were other ways to get involved. Sure enough, a week later I had another call offering me a job that was perfect for me. They had reviewed the role and decided it could be split in two; one looking at the data and one working on the people side for which they felt I would be ideal. It also meant I wouldn't need to commute to the office as often, as I could work from home for the majority of the time. Needless to say, I accepted the offer and enjoyed working on the project immensely. I'm so glad that I trusted my instincts and realised what was best for me.

Jessica – health scare

Jessica hasn't been feeling very well for a couple of weeks and she doesn't seem to be getting any better so decides that she should listen to her body and books a GP appointment (looking after her physical Health). Following some blood tests she finds out that she is pre-diabetic and if she doesn't make some changes is highly likely to develop Type 2 diabetes. Jessica sees this as a nudge to amend her lifestyle and realises she needs to start addressing some issues in her life (reviewing Your Purpose). She's been comfort eating to combat a stressful job and challenging relationship. She's been neglecting her self-care and well-being, letting her circumstances get the better of her (she realises that her Health and Mindset need improving).

Jessica becomes more mindful of what she's eating, when and why, so that she can make a conscious decision as to whether she is truly hungry or simply eating because she's feeling stressed. She also engages in more physical activity, taking a short walk on her lunch break which is not only good for her physically but also helps to improve her mental health (working on all aspects of her Health and using her Time more effectively). She tries out a local women's exercise class and, although the first session is really hard work, the group are very welcoming and encouraging, so she agrees to go again the following week. Gradually, over a period of a few weeks, her new habit of going to the class has paid off, as she can feel her fitness improving and is starting to feel more energised and motivated (building Habits for success and working on her Health). Jessica has got to know the other women and built a friendship group and they have invited her out for coffee. This helps to boost her self-confidence meaning that she feels more able to have difficult conversations at work and begins defining boundaries in her relationship (working on improving her Relationship skills).

Rita – due to retire

Rita is due to retire from her management job in a couple of months and although she is looking forward to her retirement, she's also feeling slightly anxious about how she will spend her time (remember Time can speed up or slow down depending on how we feel about something). She recognises that this is a good opportunity to review what's important to her in life and what things she would still like to do (Your Purpose). Rita feels she has many skills that could be useful and would like to make a difference in her community so she registers with her local voluntary organisation to see what's on offer (Mindset – feeling she still has something valuable to offer). She sees that the dogs' home are looking for someone to help with organising fundraising events. Rita loves animals so this is a cause close to her heart. Her management skills would be a valuable asset to the organisation and she feels that she would enjoy organising events and it would give her a sense of purpose. Rita arranges to have a chat and discuss the opportunity further as she wants to make sure it's the right fit for her and her lifestyle. She wants to ensure she still has time to go away with her husband, see her grandchildren and have time for herself, (using her Time wisely and ensuring she's conscious of Your Purpose).

Rita has always wanted to learn to speak Spanish so she finds a class and encourages her husband to go with her so they can spend quality time together and develop a shared interest (building and strengthening her Relationships). Rita also finds an exercise class for older women where she can have fun while staying active and meet other people (looking after her Health and building Relationships). Because Rita has thought about what she wants, she can manage her time and have open conversations with all the people around her to ensure boundaries are in place and still has time for herself (using her Time and Relationship skills).

I've refrained from going down the *and they all lived*

happily ever after route with the above examples because life isn't always straight forward and rosy! However, hopefully it is clear how life can be better and more enjoyable when utilising the RHYTHM principles and skills. I haven't explicitly identified where they are tapping into Mindset but they are all exhibiting a positive, growth-centric mindset through their actions. When we have the right mindset and adopt helpful habits, we can deal with any situation, even if it is uncomfortable and challenging.

When writing this book, I've encountered a few personal challenges and have had to reflect on my own choices and habits to ensure my well-being. RHYTHM is an ongoing process that never stops; we are constantly going to experience obstacles as we go through life and we can use these foundations to help us deal with them in a way that leads to personal growth.

Going forwards

Use this book, the RHYTHM wheel, and your notes and answers to the questions as a guide to changing your lifestyle. Please don't leave them in a notebook, sitting on a shelf, never to be looked at again! For true transformation you have to implement the ideas and take action. Come back to these principles whenever you need a reminder or your circumstances change, and see it as your handbook for living the life you want.

'Don't let your learning lead to knowledge.
Let your learning lead to action'
– Jim Rohn, American author and entrepreneur

Acknowledgements

It turns out that writing a book is more than just putting pen to paper, or fingers to keyboard! There are a few people who I would like to thank for their help and support in writing this book. Firstly, thank you to Amy Warren, my fantastic book coach who helped me shape my idea and guide me through the initial writing stages as part of her *Author Accelerator* programme. Her unwavering support, encouragement and nudging gave me the reassurance that I was on the right track. I would also like to thank the other ladies in the Author Accelerator group (Sue, Adelle, Jenny and Geraldine) whose camaraderie was a great help. During the early stages of writing, I ran a pilot group coaching program using the RHYTHM model to test out the content and structure for the book – thank you to the members of this group (Natalie-Claire, Dawn, Rob, Adam and Helen) who gave me valuable feedback. There were a few beta readers to check that I was on point and to spot any errors; thank you Sue Scott, Julie Howells, Leigh Phillips and my mum, Elaine, for taking the time to read through it and give feedback.

I discovered that writing the book is just the first part! There is a lot more to consider once the writing is finished and that's where it gets more technical. Thank you to Olivia Eisinger for editing my book. Nat Ravenlock at The Book Typesetters was amazing in making my book look and feel how I wanted it to; thanks for your patience and answering all my questions. Thank you Helen Bell from *Helen Bell Design* for being incredibly helpful and bringing RHYTHM to life with your graphic designs, logos, icons and book cover – it helped to bring the concept alive for me.

I'd also like to acknowledge the wisdom of other people who have influenced my journey of personal growth over the years. I've read many books, listened to podcasts, attended online and in person events and courses. And I will continue to do so, as growth is a continual process of evolution that I find fascinating. My latest growth spurt is being fuelled by the wisdom of Peter Sage. Watch this space!

References, additional resources and further reading

Over the years I've read many interesting and inspiring books that have helped me to develop my mindset and skills. I hope *RHYTHM* will be a good introduction into various topics to help give you the impetus for further development. Below are some of the resources that I've referred to and read that you may like to check out for yourself.

Books:

Brené Brown, *Atlas of the Heart*, Vermilion, 2021

Brené Brown, *Daring Greatly*, Penguin Life, 2015

James Clear, *Atomic Habits*, Random House Business, 2018

Steven R Covey, *The 7 Habits of Highly Effective People,*

Simon & Schuster UK, 1989

T. Harv Ecker, *Secrets of the Millionaire Mind: Mastering the inner game of wealth*, Harper Business, 2005

Hal Elrod, *The Miracle Morning*, Generic, 2018

Susan Jeffers, *Feel the Fear and Do It Anyway*, Ballantine Books, 1988

Gary Rolfe, Dawn Freshwater & Melanie Jasper, *Critical Reflection in Nursing and the Helping Professions: a user's guide*, Palgrave Macmillan, 2001

Peter Sage, *The Inside Track*, Influence Publishing, 2018

Jay Shetty, *Think Like a Monk*, Thorsons, 2020

Brian Tracy, *Eat That Frog*, Yellow Kite, 2013

Other resources:

5 Ways to Wellbeing: *neweconomics.org/2008/10/five-ways-to-wellbeing*

Mind: *mind.org.uk/workplace/mental-health-at-work/five-ways-to-wellbeing*

Action for Happiness: *actionforhappiness.org*

Help with financial issues and money mindset:

moneyhelper.org.uk/en   *millionairemind.live*

Jar of Life: *youtube.com/watch?v=m0hqBIugr7I*

Resources and programmes by Rebecca

Balancing Act: Maintaining a Work-Life Balance While Working from Home, bookboon.com/en/balancing-act-ebook

Self-Love Journal: Improve your Mindset in 90 days, Lulu.com, 2018

Starter For 10

JOY Day Retreats

About Rebecca

Rebecca Norton is a Life Coach, trainer and workshop facilitator from Sheffield, with a passion for the outdoors and a deep belief in the transformative power of nature. Known for her Yorkshire grit and curiosity, Rebecca has built a career around helping people develop greater self-awareness, improve their mindset, and make empowering choices that lead to fulfilling lives.

A turning point in Rebecca's journey came in 2000, when she read *Feel the Fear and Do It Anyway* by Susan Jeffers. This book opened up a whole new world of personal development, sparking her lifelong passion for self-improvement and learning.

With a diverse background that spans teaching, community development, project work and outdoor activity instruction, Rebecca's coaching is grounded in real-world experience and an unwavering commitment to personal growth. Her time spent in nature, whether walking, thinking, or simply being, has shaped not only her life but her approach to coaching. It was during a walk in the great outdoors that Rebecca first found the inspiration to become a Life Coach, believing that walking and talking outside can be a catalyst for profound change.

Rebecca was shortlisted for The Coaching Academy's Best Newcomer Award in 2018 and has continued to expand her practice through further study and regular involvement in coaching forums. Rebecca was delighted to be voted SPMG's (Supervision Plus Membership Group) Community Coach of the Year 2024. In her work, she draws on her rich blend of skills and experiences to empower individuals to lead lives they love, with a focus on self-discovery, resilience and positive action.

When she's not working, Rebecca enjoys exploring new places, walking by the coast and sharing tea and scones with family and friends. A committed member of Girlguiding for over 20 years, she lives by the motto *"Be Prepared,"* which has served her well in both her personal and professional life.

This book is a reflection of Rebecca's mission to inspire others to take action and make lasting changes in their lives; embodying Jim Rohn's principle, *'Don't let your learning lead to knowledge. Let your learning lead to action.'*

How to contact Rebecca

Website: *senseofdirection.life*

LinkedIn: *linkedin.com/in/rebeccanlifecoach*

Facebook: *facebook.com/RNSenseofdirection*